THIRD WORLD IDEOLOGY AND WESTERN REALITY

THIRD WORLD IDEOLOGY AND WESTERN REALITY

Manufacturing Political Myth

Carlos Rangel

Foreword by Jean-François Revel

*Translated by the Author
with the Assistance of Vladimir Tismaneanu,
Ralph van Roy and María Helena Contreras*

Transaction Books
New Brunswick (U.S.A.) and Oxford (U.K.)

Library of Congress Catalog Number: 85-24486
ISBN: 0-88738-601-6 (paper)
Printed in the United States of America

Library of Congress Cataloging in Publication Data

Rangel, Carlos, 1929-
  Third world ideology and Western reality.

  Translation of: El tercermundismo.
  Includes index.
  1. Developing countries. 2. Socialism—Developing
countries. 3. Capitalism—Developing countries.
I. Title.
HC59.7.R26513   1986   330.9172′4   85-24486
ISBN 0-88738-601-6 (pbk.)

Second Printing 1987

Again and always for and because of
Sofia

Contents

Foreword

Jean-François Revel

In this book Carlos Rangel analyzes an exasperating subject: most of
the governments currently dominating the planet have no interest in
reducing the inequalities between rich and poor nations. Participation
in political and ideological exploitation of these inequalities is more
advantageous to these governments than their correction; moreover,
correction of such inequalities would cause the disappearance of the
forms of power that reign over most of the Third World—forms of
power from which politicians, skilled at manipulation, derive an unusual combination of omnipotence and irresponsibility.

In the rich countries, the left, stripped of its moral horizon by the
now undeniable bankruptcy of communism, has shifted to what Carlos
Rangel calls "the Third World ideology," its ideological imagination
and its thirst for guilt comprising the sources of its desire for eternal
onmipotence. But that imagination and that thirst, as until recently the
communist illusion, do not originate from any concern for curing world
poverty in practice. The objective of the Third World ideology is to
accuse and, if possible, destroy the developed societies, not to develop
the backward societies. A specific success against underdevelopment
would imply a painful revision of the essentials of the Third World
ideology.

This attitude appears transparent in the well-known Brandt Report
on North-South relations (1980), which nowhere contemplates that the
relative poverty of the underdeveloped countries might have any other
explanation than the existence of the countries that have been able to
overcome underdevelopment. The report attributes to the "North" all
the responsibility for the backwardness of the "South" and all the
burden of the efforts to relieve these countries of their poverty.

The Soviet Union finds evident political benefit in the perpetuation
of the Third World ideology, in which it has found fertile terrain for the
rapid establishment and extension of a substantial colonial empire. In
that empire poverty reigns, as there is no reason why the Soviet Union

should be able to export a well-being that it has been unable to create within its own borders. The same is true for the other communist power, China, as demonstrated by the devastating effect of its occupation of Tibet and its protectorate over Cambodia. But what difference does it make? For communist imperialism, the essential point is that the Third World should believe in salvation through socialism before entering into the Communist bloc; and the tool of this propaganda is the complex of lies and myths impelling the underdeveloped countries to set as a priority the elimination of the influence of the advanced capitalist countries. Therein resides the explanation for North-South reports: in these documents the South is invariably pushed toward the East.

Many people find the Third World ideology beneficial—except, clearly, the people of the Third World themselves, whose opinion no one cares to seek, and who, in any case, could give it only with great difficulty, since practically all of them live under dictatorial regimes and censorship. And on top of this, it is well known that UNESCO has been trying to aid the dictators of the Third World in organizing and legitimizing a bizarre "New International Information Order," ordained to make inaccessible to the people of the Third World information about themselves and other countries, while preventing the international community from access to true information on what really is happening in countries of the Third World.

For all of these reasons, Carlos Rangel's book is probably destined to almost universal execration. Nevertheless, this book traces the only path toward understanding the problem of economic inequalities among nations, and therefore it opens the possibility of searching for true solutions to that problem.

Those solutions will not be found if initially we do not correctly answer an infrequently formulated question: What is development? And, immediately thereafter, another question: What are the causes of development? To these two questions, the Third World ideology responds: Development is wealth. If the rich countries of today are developed it is because they plundered those countries that remain poor, first by colonization and more recently by unfair exchanges, buying from them cheaply and selling to them dearly. If this diagnosis were admitted, the only way to meet the challenge of poverty would be a direct transfer of the wealth of the developed to the underdeveloped world—a sort of income tax applied to the rich nations—until the poor nations that were robbed were reimbursed.

This argument is currently accepted as virtually axiomatic. Does it have scientific bases, or rather are we confronted by a twofold fraud in which a political weapon and the death instinct are rolled into a single ideological superstructure? That is the question that lies at the center of this book. And that is the debate at the heart of our era. In his classic *The Latin Americans*[1], Carlos Rangel has already handled it with originality, depth, precision and courage in the Latin American case; now he extends his analysis to the whole class of countries known as the Third World.

Two centuries ago the whole world was underdeveloped, only it did not know it. What we now call underdevelopment was the normal condition of mankind. Most of the countries that are now developed began their take-off with considerable delay in comparison with the pioneer countries. Scarcely one hundred years ago or even less, some of the "rich" countries of this last part of the twentieth century were analogous to the "poor" countries of today, due to low per capita income, weak agricultural productivity, the short life expectancy of their inhabitants, primitive industry, the precariousness of their foreign trade. Originally it was not a generally rich world, in which some regions took the lead by the expedient of plundering others. It was a globally poor world in which some regions developed and others did not.

Now, the regions that have developed are not necessarily the ones that conquered a large number of other regions during the first modern colonial period, that corresponding in my view to the era between the eighth century A.D. and the middle of the twentieth century. It was that approximate twelve-hundred-year period that saw the conquests and annexations of which Europeans, Arabs, and Turks were the protagonists. I propose that we recognize a second modern colonial period, beginning with World War II, which witnessed the dawn of a Soviet colonial expansion destined to encompass in a short period important and extensive territories in Europe as well as in Asia, Africa, and Latin America.

During the first modern colonial period, Spain and Portugal for some centuries possessed the most extensive and richest empires; yet among all the countries of Western Europe, they have had the latest and weakest development. By contrast Germany, a classic example of a country without a significant empire, began to surpass England already by the end of the last century.

The Third World ideologue will retort that countries such as Germany, Sweden or Switzerland did not need colonies; they could and can plunder the Third World by the mechanism of unfairness in the terms of trade. But with this argument we fall into the dilemma of the chicken and the egg. Which of the two precedes the other? Without capital, without raw materials and without energy there is no possible industrial development. But without industrial development, raw material and energy have no market, no use, and no value. And let us not forget that the first industrial boom in Europe was based on coal, taken from its own underground.

As for plunder, it began in the upper paleolithic. Since then, unceasingly, the tribe has conquered and plundered other tribes, the community other communities, the nation other nations, the empire other empires. The sum total of that plunder did not give rise to development. If conquering and plundering were sufficient for development, mankind would have known development at least two thousand years ago. There is no people that have not at one time or another subjected and despoiled others, while awaiting the same fate. Nevertheless, poverty, hunger, or at best severe frugality were the fundamental characteristics in the history of human societies until the seventeenth century. The barbarians invaded and plundered the Roman Empire, but, far from developing—thanks to this booty—what they did was to extend backwardness, reverting Western Europe to a protohistoric condition.

The point is that wealth is not development. Iraq, Mexico, Indonesia, and Nigeria are rich countries, but they are not developed countries. As for the Soviet Union, it can be said that it is a great underdeveloped power characterized by backwardness of agriculture, the incapacity for taking advantage of immense mineral resources, and a very low level and quality of life coexisting with a bloated military sector and success in some military-related refined technologies. True development, on the other hand, results from a balanced synergy of factors, where intellectual liberty, the political-administrative system, relations between the state and businessmen, pluralism in the civilization and in customs, and the integrity of leaders, count as much as or more than an available capital and fitful increases in consumption.

The answer of Third World ideologues to the problem of the inequality of nations is self-contradictory. If the high economic level of developed societies were really due to theft by a handful of countries of the wealth of the majority, the problem would be hopeless. The bulk of mankind, leaving aside the ten richest nations, would never be able to grab back enough to achieve development. If, in order to obtain the results that we see in Switzerland, it had been necessary to directly or deviously despoil fifty or one hundred countries of the Third World, those fifty or one hundred countries would obtain only insignificant crumbs if all of them joined together to divide the wealth of Switzerland. The only hope of overcoming the poverty that overwhelms the majority of mankind is that the Third World ideology be wrong in its diagnosis; and that development be the result not of robbery (as it can hardly result from even the most massive transfer of resources from the rich to the poor nations), but rather of an internal process of creation, organization, administration, and growth—and, at an international level, not from plunder, but from trade.

If plunder of raw materials and inequality in the terms of trade were the explanation of development, the Soviet Union, the only present-day colonial power—while ferociously exploiting its overseas colonies and systematically practicing inequality in the terms of trade in the bosom of its European empire—should be one of the world's most advanced countries and one of the most prosperous consumer societies. But what we see there is backwardness and penury.

Carlos Rangel is further right in emphasizing and placing at the center of his argument the contention that the Third World ideology is the form that Marxism-Leninism has found to derive political benefit from the problem of underdevelopment. As long as the discussion on underdevelopment remains a weapon of Marxism-Leninism against the developed democracies, there will be no hope of relieving the poverty of the backward nations. Experience has sufficiently shown that the Marxist system is incapable of generating prosperity anywhere. In the Third World countries that have adopted it, it has not achieved, nor will it achieve, anything but setting them back further. The Soviet Union uses the Third World as a political tool for the goal of destroying the advanced capitalist countries, and it reserves for it the unenviable destiny of increasing the herd of its colonies. A supplementary illustration of this purely destructive behavior is the scandal of the so-called movement of nonaligned countries, that now is totally in the hands of Moscow's lackeys. The Soviets use the Third World for its ends in the same way that, formerly, cruel adults mutilated small children to use them as beggars. While communism remains powerful and socialism respectable, no sound, organic solution will emerge for the problem of underdevelopment.

Efficient action is not possible without correct analysis of the problem at hand. Ideological and demagogic saturation have blocked us almost completely from understanding one of the most vital issues of our time. The few authors who have treated this subject with courage have remained largely unread, even those who have achieved fame. We hope that this book by Carlos Rangel will be a significant step forward in a task of intellectual path clearing on which the destiny of so many human beings depends.

Note

1. Harcourt Brace Jovanovich, 1977.

1

Introduction

"I have seen the future and it works!" This ecstatic exclamation by the American, Lincoln Steffens, about 1920, perfectly conveys the immense hope that the first half of our century placed on socialism, once it had been established that a govenment of that tendency had managed to take hold in Russia.

With World War I, the advanced capitalist countries seemed to have given conclusive proof of their essential perversity. Even the leaders of the capitalist West had not all managed to hide that in the secret of their hearts, they more or less shared the thesis of Hobson and Lenin[1] on the inexorable imperialist nature of mature capitalism. The development of capitalist civilization had coincided with the exacerbation and the recognition of great social and political problems. Modern wars, turned into bloody tests of the most refined and specialized products of industrialism, had come to be seen not as an extension of all previous historical experience, but rather as an aberration of capitalism. And even nationalism, so much in vogue today, was perceived as an instrument of the bourgeoisie, an ideology of the dominant classes, antithetical to the humanist ideal of proletarian internationalism.

For all of this, only Marxist socialism seemed to offer an explanation and a solution. The trial against capitalism ·seemed to have been concluded with an irrefutable adverse verdict: it appeared evident that the liberal capitalist system no longer had any more to offer, nor any other reason for dragging on than the interests of the privileged classes.

On the other hand, socialism had begun to be seen as inevitable, just as Marx had argued: at once the only path toward the future and the guarantee that that future would mean a radical mutation of history, a leap from injustice, poverty, and servitude to justice, equality, and well-being. Humanism seemed definitely identified with that socialist future. To be a socialist was equivalent to being a pacifist, an internationalist, a progressive, an equalitarian, a supporter of the full development of productive forces and of the equitable sharing of wealth, a friend of liberty, an enemy of tyranny.

True Socialism

Sixty-five years later things appear quite different. Socialism has indeed been the future for a group of countries that are otherwise very dissimilar; but precisely that fact has forced an ever greater number of thoughtful people to conclude that it does not work, or at least that it works in a way quite different from what was expected. The original revolutionary protagonist, the Soviet Union, has admitted having suffered a tyranny of an inhumanity and an ignominy without precedent in the years following the Leninist application, which had been faithful to and at the same time brilliantly flexible and creative, of the fundamental Marxist propositions. And no one (least of all the adherents of Marxist philosophy) can accept the explanation, forwarded to justify that scandal, that such results were due exclusively to the aberrations of one individual.

Beyond this, the performance of Stalin's successors has been hardly less objectionable. The relaxation of tyranny since 1953 seems to have been imposed upon the leaders by circumstances alien to the socialist structures created after 1917. The timid economic reforms that have produced some positive results are heretical with respect to the socialist project, and have done no more than emphasize the inadequacy and the wrongheadedness of socialist orthodoxy. Soviet foreign policy, deprived now of the halo of axiomatic virtue that for so many years adorned all of the acts of the so-called fatherland of the workers, has revealed itself to be as imperialistic and as self-interested as that of any other great historic power, if not more so.

In short, Soviet reality seems today (and this revelation is accepted even by some communist parties in the West) as a mixture of hateful political and ideological repression and poor economic performance at home plus a brutal and voracious imperialism abroad.[2]

On the credit side, which there is no need to deny, Soviet socialism has achieved significant advances in social security, public health, and education. But it is disingenuous to argue that such achievements are characteristic or exclusive of socialism, since sundry non-socialist countries have achieved much more satisfactory levels in the same areas. In our time any reasonably well-governed and fairly prosperous country can offer its inhabitants some measure of social security, health and education; and unless it can be proved that the only way toward prosperity and good government is socialism, it is manifestly preferable to enjoy those advantages in France than in the Soviet Union.[3]

In compensation for a somber combination of tyranny, poverty, and inequalities, Soviet socialism has demonstrated itself capable of creating a formidable military machinery, a paradoxical result for a political philosophy that announced itself to be pacifist by nature. There was, it is true, the urgent necessity to defend the young revolutionary state threatened on all sides. But there is, moreover, what a posteriori seems to be a natural inclination of socialism toward militarism, the essential compatibility of a system based on universal compulsion and a centrally directed economy, with the maintenance of disproportionate armed forces, destined in large part for internal social control, but without disdaining its advantages for foreign expansion. And this in contrast with the evident repugnance of the capitalist democracies for militarism, that in them appears as a fossil survival, or, at most, as a necessary anomaly; and with the difficulty that governments encounter (France between 1918 and 1939, or western Europe after 1945) in maintaining, even in times of great prosperity—and perhaps above all during these periods—armed forces corresponding to true and present dangers.

In any case, since this unexpected trait of socialism has not damaged its image, but rather the contrary, it will have to be counted as a plus over its other scant achievements. Military power was not one of the promises of theoretical socialism—which by now ought to be qualified as naive—but in the present climate of militant nationalism and deterioration of international security, it is one of the things that nation-states most ardently desire. Therefore, the proven capacity of Marxist-Leninist socialism for militarizing a society perversely appears among the current attractions of that doctrine, and is one of the few areas in which it can be argued that it indeed works.

The Chinese Case

Countries other than the Soviet Union which have adopted socialism from 1917 on (almost invariably under foreign compulsion or, at best, as the coercive imposition of an armed minority contemptuous of democracy) have not deviated sufficiently from the Soviet norm to dissipate the reserves which by now must be harbored about socialism as a form of political, economic and social organization. In each case we encounter the usual traits of a totalitarian dictatorship founded on a bloated military apparatus and an omnipresent political police; the compulsive submission to a narrow, paralyzed and repulsive ideology;

an economy long on promises and short on achievements; and the closing of the frontiers to avoid the mass exodus of the population.

The only socialist country that, in spite of a similar depressing inventory conveys a relative sensation of net gain over its prerevolutionary situation, is China. But even in this case the friendliest observer must shudder at the revelations due to "demaoization" and the fall into disgrace of the so-called Gang of Four (commonly described in China as the Gang of Five, including Mao Tse-Tung as its first member). It is true that under communism China has been restored to the status of a respected world power. It is a moot question, however, what part of this has been due to some virtue of the socialist system and what part, on the other hand, can simply be attributed to the reestablishment in China of a central power, capable of coordinating the immense potential of a people that during millenia considered itself with some reason as the first on Earth.

The Chinese had developed an advanced level of civilization by 1200 B.C. China's great philosophers, Lao-Tsu, Confucius, Mo Ti and Mencius, lived during the Chou Dynasty, between 1122 and 249 B.C. The Great Wall, which persists in being the wonder of the world—and is in a certain way even more impressive than the spaceship Columbia—was begun by Emperor Shi Huang Ti twenty-two hundred years ago. Many of the most pleasant impressions that China travellers bring back with them are from observances of the way of cultivating land or planting trees or designing cities, and the way of life of the people— elements that have nothing to do with communism but have instead resisted the storm of the so-called Cultural Revolution, when Mao Tse Tung monstrously set out to erase China's past but succeeded only in unleashing a vast, tragic and enormously costly civil conflict.

Of course, it was no small feat on the part of Mao Tse Tung (before senility tipped him into rampant nepotism and delirious ideologism) and his associates to give their immense country a single feared and passably stable government after a century of anarchy and foreign intervention. Since Marxist ideology was the interior fire that sustained the Chinese communists in their actions, this is without doubt an important point and one worthy of careful consideration in favor of that ideology, in the same way that other religions have demonstrated equal or comparable capacities to mobilize sects that have galvanized previously lax societies throughout history.

We cannot dismiss the distressing hypothesis that in our time only Marxist-Leninist fanaticism can give power seekers the energy, but at the same time the intolerance and the cruelty necessary for indoctrinating and coercing populations with the ferocity required by certain situations. This has been, in fact, the clearest contribution of socialism to human affairs. A world ever more difficult to govern has chosen to accept antiliberty as long as it calls itself socialism, and to delude itself that a solution can thus be found to problems made even more intractable by socialist propaganda. Before the socialists gain power and radically cut all possibility for dissidence and protest, the essential point of their platform consists in declaring that those problems cannot be solved except by socialism, indeed will vanish—provided that blind faith is placed in the socialist utopia, that revolution comes, and that men resign themselves to the resulting dictatorship.

Thus, from 1917 until the present day, a score of so-called real socialisms surprisingly similar to the Soviet model (which leads one to believe that they have not only imitated that model, but rather that the same causes produce similar effects) compete over which of them is the greatest economic failure, but share a peculiar success in having established an apparently indestructible political system. Marxist-Leninist socialism bases that rock-like stability on the concentration of all power in the hands of a political-bureaucratic-police-military oligarchy; on a permanent readiness to employ any degree of repression, as broad and brutal as may be necessary; and on the monopolistic grip on the economy and the media. These last dissuade the population of any hope that there is a way out, a way back, and further deepen that hopelessness by drilling into subjects' minds the deterministic notion that inevitably the rest of the world will be sooner or later infected by the same plague.

The socialist normalization of Poland which began on 13 December 1981 is only the most recent example of the implacable operation of those mechanisms of rigid social control that the Marxist-Leninist system has been perfecting since 1917 which has smothered all libertarian whims in countries so governed until now.

Socialism and Fascism

What has happened, meanwhile, with so-called rotten capitalism? Defying all predictions, it has not ceased to function. It went through a difficult period during and after World War I, when even some of its most important political leaders harbored doubts about the viability of the system and were in a certain way socialists at heart. And with regard to the thinking class, the intellectuals, the creators, the political scientists, save rare exceptions, all sympathized with the Soviet Revolution, some in a vociferous and engaged way, others more discreetly, but all almost unanimously. That very war was judged unfairly as the greatest scandal of capitalism. From the crisis emerged two giants, bolshevism and fascism, ready to dispute the spoils of what was thought to be a finished social, political and economic order.

With the privilege of hindsight, it is easy today to perceive that Marxist-Leninist socialism and fascism were and are not essential contraries and antagonistic poles, as they themselves perhaps believed and insistently asserted (succeeding in persuading a whole generation), but rather enemy brothers. Fascism has the same statist ardor of Marxist socialism and is likewise antiliberal and therefore anticapitalist. Far from being the last shot of moribund bourgeois liberalism, it conceives itself as, and in fact is, a political philosophy of the socialist family.

Of course, there is no identity between communism and fascism, but the hypothetical essential contradiction between one and the other is a myth.[4]

To be sure, there has been a bitter and deadly opposition between fascists and communists, but not because they differ in their hostility toward liberalism and capitalist civilization. Although the new order both propose is identically based on social control—that is, state control—of the means of production, the fascist world view differs from that of the communists; wherever one of these totalitarianisms triumphs, the other will be exterminated, but the resulting political order will be essentially similar.

The differences between fascists and communists lie in their different conception about human nature and society. Therefore tactical variations rise in notions about how to realize the anticapitalist revolution and on the physiognomy of the new society. Fascists do not believe in the special destiny of the proletariat (although they are pro-worker and populist, which has been forgotten in the present-day misuse of the epithet "fascist"); and they hold that nationalism and racism, or at least xenophobia, are much more potent motors of history than the class struggle. They joyfully admit the natural aggressiveness and selfishness of human groups differentiated by culture or by physical features, by language or by skin or hair color.

Such fascist tenets result in the use of a language that, although different from the communists', refers to similar things. When communists speak of removing from work its mercantile character, fascists say that they are going to break the slavery of usury. Communists hold the bourgeoisie responsible for all social evils; the Nazis, sharply conscious of the power of nationalism, channeled the same social resentment against a so-called nonnational or antinational group, the Jews.

It is not by accident that Dr. Joseph Goebbels hesitated a while between communism and national-socialism. He clearly realized that both were equally compatible with his personal inclination for a radical nationalist and authoritarian government that would rescue his country from what he saw as the decadent liberalism of the Weimar Republic. For the majority of sympathizers of Marxist-Leninist socialism not as astute as Goebbels, it appeared about 1935 that there was an abysmal difference between equalitarian, progressive humanist, internationalist, antimilitaristic, proletarian, pacifist socialisms on the one hand, and reactionary, meritocratic, racist, sectarian, nationalist, plutocratic, militaristic, bellicose fascisms on the other.

But today, we are constantly being told that we must admire the military prowess of the socialist countries, we see the confusion between socialism and militant nationalism being assiduously cultivated, and the two most important socialist countries, the Soviet Union and China, are mortal enemies clearly and simply because even though they are both socialist they are geopolitical rivals. Under the ever more tenuous disguise of the Marxist ideology, both have developed and made an effort to maintain and extend spheres of imperial influence. Given this, we can appreciate that the error of Adolf Hitler (fatal for him, fortunate for the world) was to confront Marxism instead of adopting it. His passionate ambition was to turn Germany into the number one world power by means of military might and territorial conquest. If he had pursued that objective in the name of international socialism rather than national socialism, history would have taken a different course. All who admire the virtues of Germany but who fear its temptations must thank providence for having seen that the Marxist gospel did not fall first in the hands of the German state, since we know today to what extent Marxism, transfigured into an ideology, can be adapted to the uses and goals of the most classical dictatorial and imperialist militarism and serve as foundation of antiequalitarian and regimented societies.

Actually, what effectively kept Germany from making national use of its Marxist patrimony (for which an adequate leader, different from Hitler, would have eventually emerged) was the accidental fact that that political philosophy had by then become the state religion of a neighboring country that was and is Germany's historical enemy, and was therefore, since 1917, inextricably linked with the goals of the Russian nation. Under those conditions, the German experiment with totalitarian temptation and radical antiliberalism could not take place in the name of the class struggle and proletarian internationalism, but by appealing to other passions (ultranationalism, militarism, and anti-

Semitism) today integrated by Marxist-Leninist socialism with an ease that cannot be fortuitous.

From a certain point of view, fascism is a kind of essential socialism, a Machiavellian socialism that does not base its reaction against liberalism on the utopia of a classless society and the transformation of human nature. It understands that the liberal polity can best be overwhelmed by appealing to the most primary passions of human groups: xenophobia, the taste for violence, the cult of the leader; and that even then, the newly born socialist polity will only be able to sustain itself by the terrorist use of power, the totalitarian organization of society and its horizontal division according to a rigid hierarchization and specialization—a system in which the level of submission or the greater or lesser rank in the single party will determine even which young persons will receive higher education.

Meanwhile Capitalism . . .

In any case, the challenge of communist and fascist messianic collectivisms, even on top of the great depression plus a second world war much more world wide and destructive than the first, not only failed to destroy capitalism, but was one of the catalysts of the period of greatest growth and achievement of capitalist civilization since the Industrial Revolution.

The character of advance without precedent in human affairs of that first flourishing of capitalism has rarely been described with greater eloquence than by Marx and Engels in the *Communist Manifesto*.[5] Of course, Marx's and Engels' recognition of the creativity of capitalism is accessory to their contention that by 1848 that creativity was exhausted. Today we know that whatever may be the future of capitalist industrial society, if it stumbles it will not be for having reined back the productivity of human society, but rather the contrary: for having so unchained it that technological advance, production, and consumption have soared to a point where it may be feared that they could become self defeating. The limits of capitalist growth threaten to be not the choking of the productive forces, as Marx and Engels thought but rather, inversely, the excess of the productive forces liberated by the market economy in relation to the physical resources of the planet.

This is why a novel socialist argument has come up to make up for the bankruptcy of the classic Marxist thesis about the inevitable strangling of productive forces in the capitalist economy. Amazingly, coming from such quarters, it consists in the reproach that capitalism produces too much, so that socialism will be indispensible not for producing more with less effort and total liberty (as Marx argued) but rather for enforcing universal austerity and thus saving the ecological equilibrium of the planet.

Whatever their viewed advantages may be, in the form of the absence of restraints on compulsion and repression, it is doubtful whether closed societies (as, demonstrably, are the socialist societies) are more capable than open capitalist societies in responding to the myriad problems and challenges raised by the realization that the environment will not suffer uncontrolled industrial growth, or that nonrenewable and especially energy resources are much scarcer than any one had foreseen. On the contrary, the type of despotic government, uncontrolled by a free press, at once all-powerful and irresponsible, that invariably has arisen from the implantation of Marxist-Leninist socialism is unconducive to the best utilization of natural resources and respect for nature, and manifestly lacks the creativity required for innovation in research and technological development, lacking even minimum sensitivity for prudent and humane use of technology created by the West.[6]

A government such as that of the Soviet Union, comptemptuous of public opinion, can coldly and without rejoinder make what are perhaps terribly mistaken decisions, as could be the proliferation of nuclear energy plants, while in the West the open examination and free debate on this question has forced the search for alternatives. Industrial society, whether capitalist or socialist (the latter, in practice, fed almost exclusively by technologies, methods and goals copied from capitalism) runs the risk, in no way ideological but rather inherent in industrialism, of stumbling over objective obstacles to growth. If such obstacles can be overcome through the frequently demonstrated and perhaps inexhaustible human capacity for discovering, through science and technology, answers to seemingly insoluble problems, surely this will not happen in the sterile socialist societies, but rather in the protean and endlessly creative capitalist civilization.

The Fifty Years After 1928

The creativity and persistent capacity for innovation and performance of capitalist civilization were never more dazzling than in the years following World War II, when it surpassed the most optimistic calculation of the friendliest economists. Joseph Schumpeter, still in the gloomy and pervasively anticapitalist mood caused by the ongoing Great Depression, about 1940 wrote almost apologetically for suggesting that the economy of the United States could eventually, in spite of everything, in the long run (the fifty years following 1928) maintain an average growth similar to that achieved in the sixty years between 1870 and 1930.[7]

If such an extravagant development were to unfold, by 1978 the annual per capita income in the United States would have reached the unbelievable sum of $1,300! Naturally, it would have been the highest in the world, corresponding to a level of prosperity qualitatively different from anything ever reached before in history. Extreme poverty such as the majority of mankind had invariably known and suffered would have been (according to Schumpeter) virtually abolished "except in pathological cases." All the demands ever formulated by social reformers, "including the lunatics," either would have become automatically met or could have been satisfied by the state without tampering for this purpose with the mainsprings of the capitalist economic system.

We all know what has really happened. Per capita income, not only in the United States, but also without exception in all other capitalist economies, reached in short order, and then—even adjusting for inflation—surpassed many times over Schumpeter's optimistic projection. Even though we have considered per capita income as adjusted for inflation, let us not forget that many things today are not more but less expensive, in equal monetary units, thanks to the capitalist use of technology and, above all, to the large-scale production of consumer goods characteristic of the capitalist economy. For the same reason, many desirable goods that have improved the quality of life, unavailable at any price in 1940, are now obtainable in the market. And we are not merely referring to consumerism (a malicious connotation that socialists, ashamed by the low productivity of the economies of that tendency, have ended up by successfully tagging on to the category, in principle neutral, of consumption); we refer also to advances that include such basic areas as the production, conservation and distribution of food, the new technologies of medical diagnosis and treatment, and a formidable panoply of new medicines.

Have all problems therefore been solved? Of course not. Even the most penetrating thinkers run grave risks when they enter into prophecy (and even into forecasting). Marx and Engels are the most noteworthy case. Schumpeter underestimated the productive capacity of capitalism, but at the same time, naively, the demands that social reformers, not necessarily lunatic, may bring up and legitimately formulate once primary material necessities become satisfied. In the advanced capitalist countries, where there previously existed extreme poverty, poor health due to malnutrition or the lack of medical attention, unemployment without compensation, children without schools, domestic slavery of women, destitute old age, now we see disillusionment with industrial civilization, confusion and social disintegration, excessive growth of cities, and environmental contamination. In many cases these and other problems already existed before 1940, but they were secondary or went unnoticed in the face of the far more pressing matters of poverty and general scarcity. Environmental degradation, for example, obsesses prosperous societies, but is seldom or never recognized as a problem where unsatisfied human demands are the first concern. The problems of advanced capitalism are not those of poverty but rather of abundance, the result of having too much and not of greatly lacking, of overeating not starvation.[8]

It will be said that excess consumption can be, and is perhaps, the greatest problem that has arisen in human society, and the greatest threat to those countries that have achieved it due to runaway capitalist productivity. This is possible, but would be an anticapitalist argument totally different from the Marxist objections. Meanwhile, it has been demonstrated that capitalist economies are incomparably more productive and creative in all fields than the socialist economies; and moreover, that the countries where the market economy has been allowed to function during an extended period and not too imperfectly, are the same where we find variable but uniformly estimable levels of political democracy and a tendency to formulate, admit, and begin to satisfy demands that conform, paradoxically, to some of the promises of theoretical socialism. It is in the capitalist societies that have developed all the new definitions of liberty and human dignity: the rights of minorities, of women; the relaxation of the tyranny of foremen and office bosses; the liberation of the young, ecologism, unorthodox lifestyles, sexual freedom. If we look up, for example, the famous passage of the *Communist Manifesto* on sexuality and marriage in bourgeois society[9], we will find nothing corresponding to the present norm in any advanced capitalist country. On the other hand, hypocrisy and frustration in sexual relations seem to be the invariable norm in the societies that call themselves socialist.[10]

Capitalism, Socialism and the Third World

Without exception, all the countries that call themselves socialist know variable levels of economic backwardness, and all have a dismaying level of political backwardness, the first, visible and detectable to any neutral observer, and even more so to any student of their own suspect statistics; and the second, so scandalous that in recent years it has become the chief concern and subject of controversy of those sympathizers of the Marxist political philosophy who have the luck of living outside the socialist camp.

Now, the argument is well known according to which poor peoples do not aspire to liberty, and that, in any case, respect for human rights is a luxury reserved for the already developed societies. Such a proposition is highly debatable and even scandalous, but we will let it be for the time being. On the other hand, the anticapitalist argument that consists of pointing out the excess of material wealth and the consumerist character of contemporary capitalism, should not overly impress the people of the so-called Third World, who suffer from the inverse situation, and should be very happy to accept the "scourge of prosperity," such as the advanced capitalist countries suffer it, instead of the scourge of poverty that they know so well.

This being the case, only the most dogmatic anticapitalists will regard as normal the lack of prestige in the Third World of the only political and economic system that in human experience has been capable of raising the productivity of societies above the level of subsistence not only for the privileged, but for everyone, and subsequently to the astounding heights that we have seen in our lives. We could understand that the correlation of prosperity with liberty might pass unnoticed by human masses who are suffering from hunger, but not prosperity itself. Nevertheless, that is what happens, and there is hardly a leader of the so-called Third World who does not proclaim himself to be anticapitalist, and, if not Marxist-Leninist, at least democratic socialist or Christian socialist. Why this nonsense? And where does this tendency lead? The attempt to answer those questions is the purpose of this book.

Notes

1. "I was in East End of London yesterday and attended a meeting of the unemployed. I listened to the wild speeches, which were just a cry of 'bread,' 'bread,' and on my way home I pondered over the scene and I became more than ever convinced of the importance of imperialism. . . . My cherished idea is a solution for the social problem, i.e., in order to save the 40,000,000 inhabitants of the United Kingdom from a bloody civil war, we colonial statesmen must acquire new lands to settle the surplus population, to provide new markets for the goods produced by them in the factories and mines. The Empire, as I have always said, is a bread and butter question. If you want to avoid civil war, you must become imperialists." (Cecil Rhodes quoted by Lenin in his *Imperialism: The Highest Stage of Capitalism, Selected Works,* 2 vols. [Moscow: Foreign Language Publishing House, 1947], vol. 1, p. 687.)

2.   A complete state monopoly inevitably entails servitude and compulsory conformism. Each person is completely dependent upon the state. In periods of stress this servitude engenders terrorism, and in calmer times it encourages a bungling bureaucracy, mediocrity, and apathy.

Without question, we do not have the world's highest labor productivity, nor is there any hope of overtaking the developed capitalist countries in the foreseeable future. What we have is a permanent militarization of the economy to an unprecedented degree for peacetime—something that is burdensome for the population and dangerous for the whole world. What we have is chronic economic stress: a lack of reserves despite all our natural resources—the black-earth belt, coal, crude oil, timber, diversity of climate—and despite a low density of population.

It is especially significant that with resources like ours, after fifty-eight years of gigantic efforts, including thirty years of uninterrupted peace, we have nothing even faintly resembling the world's highest standard of living. A worker from any developed capitalist country—not just the United States but also, say, France, West Germany, Italy, Switzerland, etc.—would not consider working for the kind of wages we pay or with our level of protection of workers' rights. In the USSR the minimum monthly wage is 60 rubles, and the average wage is 110 rubles. In terms of purchasing power, that minimum wage amounts to about $30 a month, or 150 new French francs, while the average wage amounts to about $55 or 275 francs. Compare these figures with American standards: The average monthly wage is $600 to $800 per month; and a monthly income of $400 for a family consisting of father, mother, and two children is the official poverty threshold. For lower income levels, the state provides special benefits that a Soviet citizen could not even dream of in other countries—like France, Italy, or West Germany—the wages are somewhat lower than in the United States, but the cost of living is also lower. In the USSR, people who live on their wages spend most of them on food. If he were to read about this, an American worker—who as a rule spends no more than 25 percent of his wages in food (of much better quality), and whose wife does not work if she doesn't have to—would no doubt find it wildly improbable. (Andrei Sakharov, *My Country and the World* [New York: Knopf, 1975].)

3. In addition, it is necessary to closely examine and analyze the argument that Marxist-Leninist socialism guarantees an appreciable sum of social advantages, whatever may be their political costs. The Soviet Union is the original socialist country, of which we are told that from very early on it demonstrated the benefits of that system at the social level. Sakharov (ibid.) offers the following comments on that claim:

• Soviet workers get only two weeks paid vacation a year, and the opportunity is decided by whim of the administration.
• The work week, without overtime, is forty-one hours.
• The right of the workers to strike does not exist, nor does the right to make requests and organized claims to the authorities. For years the fishermen of Murmansk have been fighting against the merciless undervaluation of their production and against the necessity to bribe bureau-

crats to obtain fishing permits. But the only result has been repression against those who appear to be the organizers of these timid protests. Equally frustrated have been the aspirations of the Soviet workers to improve industrial security in the mines and in the chemical products factories. Security precautions in industry are widely neglected.

• Pensions and other benefits continue to be derisible, in spite of certain improvements under Khrushchev and Brezhnev. Apart from "special" and military pensions, the maximum monthy stipend is 120 rubles ($60) while the average is half. Until recently pensions were not provided for the members of collective farms, and those that exist today are minimal. The widow and children of a suicide do not receive the pension corresponding to the loss of the family head. The subsidy for the mothers of many children (a subsidy begun only during World War II) is far short of covering the corresponding burden. Single mothers are discriminated against and receive only 5 rubles monthly for each child.

• Each year the government declares a certain number of Saturdays and Sundays as work days. These so-called communist Saturdays and Sundays are theoretically optional, but woe to those who try not to work on those days! Besides, those days of "voluntary" work are not paid.

• Housing conditions are deplorable. Moreover, it is not true that housing is cheap if the cost per square meter of tiny housing units, without kitchen or private bathroom, is measured in relation to real salaries.

• The water supply is chronically scarce. Even in certain favored cities there is a perennial scarcity of food and durable goods. Bread is poor and contains additives. Availability of meat is almost nonexistent. There are serious electric and domestic gas deficits. The majority of cities and towns lack adequate sewer systems.

• The quality of education is poor, especially in rural areas. Classrooms are small and dark. Organized school transportation, so common in the West, practically does not exist. School lunches are bad. The concept of free education does not include food, uniforms, or text books. There are numerous deliberate injustices in admission to higher education. It is well known that Jews are discriminated against, but so are students of certain other nationalities, those from rural areas, the children of believers and dissidents, and generally all of those who lack "contacts." The best demonstration of the deterioration of the educational system is the growing anti-intellectualism of Soviet society.

• Medical attention for the majority of the population is of poor quality. One must stand in interminable lines to see a doctor, and when one finally gains access to the doctor, the examination is cursory. The patient cannot choose his doctor. In hospitals, there are patients lying in corridors. There is a deficit of graduate and practical nurses, of bedclothes, medicine, and food. A typical hospital receives less than one ruble per day per patient for all of its expenditures, although there are privileged hospitals that receive fifteen rubles per patient. It is not whimsical that foreign men residing in Moscow (the best served of all the Soviet cities) send their wives to give birth in capitalist countries, in spite of the fact that the medical service available to foreigners is incomparably superior to what Soviet citizens can obtain. In the provinces, modern medicine is almost unknown. Even Moscow is considerably backward compared to the West—although this does not apply for certain special hospitals and clinics, reserved for the "new class." It is prohibited to receive medicines by mail from abroad; doctors are prohibited from prescribing such medicines, and even from mentioning their existence. Medical equipment corresponds to the nineteenth century. The system of medical education has seriously deteriorated. The unquestionable advances achieved by health services in the first decades of the Soviet regime have been lost, especially in pediatrics and preventive medicine. (An unexpected confirmation of Sakharov's affirmations is found in Soviet statistics: "In the worst moments of the Stalinist period, the decline in the infant mortality rate was one of the great achievements of the regime. . . . From 1971 that evolution toward a decrease was inverted, replaced by a steady increase. . . . from 22.6 (for each one thousand children born alive) to 27.7. In comparison, in France the infant mortality rate has continued falling with regularity: from 20.7 in 1967 to 10.6 in 1978. From 1974, the Soviet Union *stopped publishing* this tremendously significant statistic, by which they confessed that the process of sanitary deterioration has continued, only denying Western observers the possibility of measuring its dimension. It is evident that the rise in the infant mortality rate reveals a collapse of the Soviet medical and food system." Emmanuel Todd, "L'URSS en Afganistan: la chute finale?", *Politique Internationale* 8 (Summer 1980):115-16.

• The very low real income means that the salary of a man is not sufficient to maintain a family, even in the case of a couple with a single child. This implies the destruction of the health of millions of women who must work outside the home and moreover are in charge of household chores.
• The most eloquent symptom of the Soviet social pathology is the tragic alcoholism of the overwhelming masses of population, including women and teenagers.

4. Affinities between fascism and bolshevism were readily admitted by both in the twenties, without qualms and with considerable mutual admiration. Gorki, in an interview for *Corriere de la Sera* given just after Mussolini had won the 1924 elections (he had had dictatorial powers since 1922), had this to say: "Observing [Mussolini's] manner of governing [directly, since Gorki at that time lived in Capri] I have learned to admire his energy; but I would rather quote Trotsky's opinion: 'Mussolini has accomplished a revolution, he is our best disciple!'" As for Lenin, he addressed a delegation of Italian socialists visiting Moscow after the fascist march on Rome (1922), saying, "What a waste that we lost Mussolini. He is a first rate man who would have led our party to power in Italy." George P. Urban, "Mussolini and Lenin: A Conversation with Domenico Settembrini," *Survey* vol. 23, no. 3 (Summer 1977-78).

5. For example:

The bourgeoisie, historically, has played a most revolutionary part. The bourgeoisie has disclosed how it came to pass that the brutal display of vigour in the Middle Ages, which Reactionists so much admire, found its fitting complement in the most slothful indolence. It has been the first to show what man's activity can bring about. It has accomplished wonders far surpassing Egyptian pyramids, Roman aqueducts, and Gothic cathedrals; it has conducted expeditions that put in the shade all former Exoduses of nations and crusades.

The bourgeoisie, by the rapid improvement of all instruments of production, by the immensely facilitated means of communication, draws all, even the most barbarian, nations into civilisation. The cheap prices of its commodities are the heavy artillery with which it batters down all Chinese walls, with which it forces the barbarians' intensely obstinate hatred of foreigners to capitulate. It compels all nations, on pain of extinction, to adopt the bourgeois mode of production; it compels them to introduce what it calls civilisation into their midst, i.e., to become bourgeois themselves. In one word, it creates a world after its own image.

The bourgeoisie has subjected the country to the rule of the towns. It has created enormous cities, has greatly increased the urban population as compared with the rural, and has thus rescued a considerable part of the population from the idiocy of rural life. Just as it has made the country dependent on the towns, so it has made barbarian and semi-barbarian countries dependent on the civilised ones, nations of peasants on nations of bourgeois, the East on the West.

The bourgeoisie, during its rule of scarce one hundred years, has created more massive and more colossal productive forces than have all preceding generations together. Subjection of Nature's forces to man, machinery, application of chemistry to industry and agriculture, steam-navigation, railways, electric telegraphs, clearing of whole continents for cultivation, canalisation of rivers, whole populations conjured out of the ground—what earlier century had even a presentiment that such productive forces slumbered in the lap of social labour? (Karl Marx and Frederick Engels, "Manifesto of the Communist Party," in Karl Marx and Frederick Engels, *Selected Works,* 2 vols. [Moscow: Foreign Language Publishing House, 1956] vol. 1.)

6.   The consequences of the Party-State monopoly are especially destructive in the sphere of culture and ideology. The complete unification of ideology at all times and places—from the school desk to the professorial chair—demands that people become hypocrites, timeservers, mediocre, and stupidly self-deceiving. The tragicomic, ritualistic farce of the loyalty oath is played over and over, relegating to the background all considerations of practicality, common sense, and human dignity. Writers, artists, actors, teachers, and scholars are under such monstrous ideological pressure that one wonders why art and the humanities have not altogether vanished in our country. The influence of those same anti-intellectual factors on the exact sciences and the applied sciences is more indirect but no less destructive. A comparison of scientific, technological and economic achievements in the USSR and abroad makes this perfectly plain. It is no accident that for many years, in our country, new and promising scientific trends in biology and cybernetics could not develop normally, while on the surface out-and-out demagogy, ignorance, and charlatanism bloomed like gorgeous flowers. It is no accident that all the great scientific and technological

discoveries of recent times—quantum mechanics, new elementary particles, uranium fission, antibiotics and most of the new, highly effective drugs, transistors, electronic computers, the development of highly productive strains in agriculture, the discovery of other components of the "Green Revolution," and the creation of new technologies in agriculture, industry, and construction—all of them happened outside our country.

The significant achievements in the first decade of the space age, which were due to the personal qualities of the late Academician S. P. Korolev and to certain fortuitous features of our programs for building military rockets, which made possible their direct use in space— constitute an exception which does not disprove the rule. And certain successes in military technology are the result of an enormous concentration of resources in that sphere. (Sakharov, *My Country and the World.*)

7. J. A. Schumpeter, *Capitalism, Socialism and Democracy* New York: Harper & Brothers, 1962).

8. That situation, in which there is unprecedented production and consumption, persists almost unchanged in the advanced capitalist countries in spite of the tenfold increase in oil prices since 1973. The example of having withstood such a setback without collapse is perhaps even better proof of the vitality and flexibility of capitalism than the explosive growth shown in the immediately previous years.

9.   On what foundation is the present family, the bourgeois family, based? On capital, on private gain. In its completely developed form this family exists only among the bourgeoisie. But this state of things finds its complement in the practical absence of the family among the proletarians, and in public prostitution.

The bourgeois family will vanish as a matter of course when its complement vanishes, and both will vanish with the vanishing of capital.

But you Communists would introduce community of women, screams the whole bourgeoisie in chorus.

The bourgeois sees in his wife a mere instrument of production. He hears that the instruments of production are to be exploited in common, and, naturally, can come to no other conclusion than that the lot of being common to all will like-wise fall to the women.

He has not even a suspicion that the real point aimed at is to do away with the status of women as mere instruments of production.

For the rest, nothing is more ridiculous than the virtuous indignation of our bourgeois at the community of women which, they pretend, is to be openly and officially established by the Communists. The Communists have no need to introduce community of women; it has existed almost from time immemorial.

Our bourgeois, not content with having the wives and daughters of their proletarians at their disposal, not to speak of common prostitutes, take the greatest pleasure in seducing each others' wives.

> Bourgeois marriage is in reality a system of wives in common and thus, at the most, what the Communists might possibly be reproached with, is that they desire to introduce, in substitution for a hypocritically concealed, an openly legalised community of women. (Marx and Engels, "Manifesto of the Communist Party.")

10. An illuminating work on this topic is by Dr. Mikhail Stern, *Sexual Life in the USSR* (Paris: Albin Michel, 1979). The table of contents reads in part: "From the 'socialization of the woman' to the 'communist family.' Sex, the enemy of the revolution. Stalinist virtue. The modern Soviet family. How is love made in the USSR? The result of puritanism. The loss of sexual appetite. Frigidity and impotence, national scourges. Exhibitionism and voyeurism. Sexual relations in public places. Prostitution. Prostitution in prisons and concentration camps. Prostitution with foreigners. Sexual violence against minors. Alcoholism and criminality. Masculine and feminine homosexuality. Sexual life in the concentration camps."

2

What Is Socialism?

The word *socialism* was used for the first time in France or England around 1830, but the socialist spirit is eternal. Among the persistent components of socialist thought and feeling is the conviction that there exists an intractable contradiction between collective interests and the selfishness of individuals. There is a very short, and very easily negotiated distance between this idea and the incarnation of the community in the state, supposedly concerned only with the general welfare, impersonal, disinterested, virtuous and wise, in contrast with the regrettable selfishness of flesh and blood human beings.

Unfortunately, the political practices carried out under the label *socialist* have been very far removed from the hopes placed in the illusion of the superhuman state. This is clearly evident in the countries where regimes reign inspired in that "perfect socialism" that is Marxism-Leninism; and still more painfully so in the so-called Third World, where any armed minority that can seize power and dedicate itself to oppressing the population and ruining the economy finds it advantageous to do so in the name of socialism.

As a result, socialist political philosophy has had to undergo strange fractures and distortions. It could not be otherwise, as it is invoked by regimes such as those of India, Algeria, North Korea, Tanzania, Albania, Cuba, and Cambodia. Of the nearly twenty African states that declare themselves to be socialist, no fewer than twelve have pretensions to be "scientific socialists," among them Angola, Ethiopia, and Congo-Brazzaville.

In order to claim that socialism is being built, it is enough that a tiny group seize the state in a sovereign territory, declare itself socialist, and begin to receive weapons from the Soviet Union, whatever may be the previous development of productive forces in that territory. At first glance this would appear to be a semantical disaster, a confusion that can only guarantee the failure of every attempt to significantly employ the word *socialism*. Nevertheless, the currently and universally accepted use of the word corresponds to a solid core of meaning. There is an essential truth in what is in appearance a purely verbal adherence to socialism on the part of regimes that in some cases have not even passed beyond the stage of tribalism.

Similarly, all self-identified socialists do know more or less what goal they seek, although not all pursue it with equal vigor or ferocity. There is something in common between Joseph Stalin and Indira Gandhi, so that an imaginary net held by these two characters would have room not only for the so-called socialist camp (the subset or subspecies which I have referred to as perfect socialist) but also, without any difficulty, for those as diverse as Nehru, Nasser, Nkruma, Bumedienne, Nyerere, Che Guevara, Sekou Ture, and in general a large proportion of political leaders of the Third World after 1945—and, of course, for the socialist politicians of the West.

Famous intellectuals and artists would also swim into our net, such as Sartre, Marcuse, Harold Laski, Moravia, Cortázar; but also an immense multitude of insignificant writers, painters, professors, actors, and journalists, a fauna along the fringes of original intellectual and high creative activitity, who blame the mediocrity of their lives on capitalist society and think they will get their revenge come the socialist revolution.

Snugly lodged in the net is a sector of the church, not only priests, but also lay Catholics who cross the poorly defined frontier between Christian democracy and Christian socialism. And, finally, a number of people who are confused, dissatisfied or overwhelmed by sensations of guilt, among them not a few successful businessmen, manifest incarnations of hated capitalism.

A Reactionary Nostalgia

Socialism, or more generally the socialist spirit, is by no means a superior stage or a progress in relation to what is today known as capitalism, but rather a reaction, a reactionary reflex, a visceral rejection of the social, cultural, economic and political consequences of the market economy. In the case of the Third World countries, there is the added ingredient of a very understandable grudge toward a world economic system within which those countries have suffered not from a uniformly harmful foreign impact, as is argued, but rather from one that has been uniformly humiliating and traumatic. Third World regions have endured forced recruitment into the world capitalist order, and have seen the success and great power of the original capitalist countries within that order contrasted with their own persistent poverty and weakness.

Pierre Leroux (1797-1871) claims to have been the first to use the term *socialism* as a "necessary neologism in contra-distinction to Individualism."[1] He explains that this latter term describes a condition of society, induced by the rise of the industrial and financial economy, characterized by the destruction of the traditional social fabric. Within this new condition of society, the individual must look out for his or her own interests. "Individualists," writes Leroux, "base themselves on the principle that government should serve only as policeman . . . and limit its function to the regulation of the differences between individuals, within the ongoing order of property and inheritance. In this way property becomes the only remaining basis of human society. Unfortunately, the result of such casting aside all social providence is that the share of some tends always to increase, and that of others to always decrease, so that the system leads to the most vile inequality. The liberty that it proclaims is a lie, because very few enjoy it, and because, as a consequence of inequality, society becomes a battlefield between thieves and their victims, a breeding ground of vice, suffering, immorality, and crime."[2]

Those few words show how little Marx and Engels added to the essential anticapitalist argument. And Leroux's critique is all the more significant since Leroux himself was not exactly enraptured by socialism. He quite clearly perceived, at the same time as the iniquities of savage liberalism, the totalitarian vocation of socialism, "whose adherents march defiantly toward what they call an organic epoch, and are already concerned with the means and ways they are going to use to bury all liberty and all spontaneity under what they describe as organization. Ask them how they will be able to reconcile liberty with authority, and what to do, for example, with freedom of expression, and they will answer that society is a great Being, whose functions should not be perturbed by anyone."[3]

The foundation of socialism, the substance of the mesh of that imaginary net, held between Stalin and Indira Gandhi, is the instinctive and spontaneous repugnance of every human being—virtually without exception—toward the capitalist liberal economy based on private property, inequality, and inheritance; and where human beings, in the absence of efficient legal provision to protect them, tend to be considered as objects according to their function in production, like land, plants, animals, minerals, and machinery.

Other fibers of the net are a strong skepticism with relation to the civil and political rights guaranteed by liberalism ("the liberty that it proclaims is a lie'') and a general repugnance toward the social atmosphere, the environment of capitalism with its necessary inequality, its merciless individualism, and a state of constant competition that results in the almost sure failure of the less well trained, and the correlative success, likewise predetermined, of the well fed and well educated. And there is the added paradox that these latter are not therefore necessarily happy or even comfortable, since the essence of capitalism is that there are no definitively acquired social positions (as with nobility, or in fact any other social status within feudalism). Rather, wealth or prestige not only can be dissipated without leaving a trace, but cannot even remain static without being tarnished, if those who have achieved or inherited them do not remain dynamic and capable.

Thus, for the majority of human beings the net effect of living in a competitive society with social mobility and freedom, is an agonizing sensation, similar to that of the swimmer who can never touch bottom and must make a constant effort to remain afloat.

The Abolition of Private Property

A corollary is inevitable. If we accept the premise of the socialist spirit (according to which the social organization and the cultural environment of capitalist civilization are intolerable) which wishes to block capitalist development where there exists a precapitalist or backward capitalist order, or to abolish it and "go beyond" capitalism where it has already yielded its utmost (this last being the orthodox Marxist thesis), one must aim at its heart, which is private property.

For this reason and contrary to a widely held but wrong belief, Sweden is not a truly socialist country, because the greater part of the means of production of that country (including the banks and insurance companies) remain private property. What Sweden has done is to tax to the limit (probably beyond the prudent limit) the profits of notably efficient and productive capitalist companies, as well as to virtually confiscate personal income above a likewise too stringent norm, and thus to finance a vast and relatively well administered social security program.

It is disingenuous to claim that this system is a variant of the type of political regime that in a totalitarian way dominates every aspect of life in countries such as the Soviet Union, Vietnam or Cuba. Those who so argue are deceiving themselves (and are ridiculed by the so-called true socialists, the Marxist-Leninists, who in the same way disqualify even the Yugoslavian model); or perhaps they hope to deceive others making them believe that if only socialism is put into practice in a correct way, avoiding the errors and deviations that supposedly have adulterated it wherever it has been tried, its condition sine qua non (absent in Sweden) which is the abolition of private property, need not generate totalitarianism but rather will be compatible and even consubstantial with freedom and democracy.

To be a socialist is to believe in the abolition of private ownership of the means of production. The socialist countries are the ones that have taken that step. Those who, while thinking of themselves as socialists, do not share that belief; or who, having governed, have not tried to expropriate the means of production, are not genuine socialists. Rather, they have been restrained by circumstances in their desire to establish true socialism, and have had to content themselves with merely restrictive (and not destructive) measures against private economic activity, in the hope that in this way they are somehow bringing closer the grand day when capitalism can be finally erased from the face of the earth.

Such has been the case of the socialist parties of Western Europe, including of course the Swedish party, but also the British and French parties. Somewhat different is the case of the Social Democratic Party in West Germany, which no longer claims to be a socialist party and is not ashamed to call itself social democrat.

Social Democracy and Democratic Socialism

This distinction is nonexistent to Marxist-Leninists, who find equally reformist and social democratic all parties that do not use so-called democratic centralism in their internal affairs; do not accept the essential virtue of the Soviet system (or at least the theory of "positive bottom line" of seventy years of bolshevism); and do not see the Soviet Union as a country that is "building socialism and advancing toward communism." And perhaps it is the Marxist-Leninists who are right. Olof Palme, Tony Wedgewood-Benn and François Mitterrand can be very radical in their statements in comparison with Helmut Schmidt, Mario Soares, Felipe González or Bettino Craxi, but while holding power they have not attempted any Leninist coup, nor is it probable that they would ever attempt one, as did communist Alvaro Cunhal in Portugal as soon as he believed that he had a chance of success.

The fact is that socialists self-identified as democratic and social democrats are both sincerely committed to maintaining the so-called bourgeois freedoms. Therefore they must proceed in a reformist and "non-revolutionary" way when they accede to power, which moreover they obtain within "bourgeois" legality through elections that place certain levers in their hands—but not the totality of power. Nevertheless, in sundry ways they have widened the areas of direct intervention of the state in the lives of their respective nations. They have inordinately raised taxes, and not only those of the coupon clipping idle rich and of high-salaried managers of giant corporations, but also those of ordinary people; and sometimes, as in Sweden and Great Britain, to fantastic levels, precisely to finance the growth and reach of the state not only in undisputed areas such as social security, public health, and free elementary education, but in everything.

Finally, the democratic socialists and social democrats have ended up by extending the jurisdiction and the direct powers of the state to such an extent and with such foolish pretense of skill in planning the economy, that they may indeed have gone some way toward preparing the fall of their societies into socialism, not by civil war or by a Leninist coup d'etat, as Marxist-Leninists propose, but rather by the gradual reduction, first slow then swift, of the breathing space of the market economy and therefore of political liberty.

We find ourselves then with a paradox. Democratic socialists and social democrats have earned (and deserve), on the one hand, the gratitude of liberal democrats, who esteem their devotion to political liberty while deploring their failure to realize that it is inseparable from the market economy. Liberal democrats admit, moreover, that without trade union organization of socialist or social democratic inspiration, capitalism would not have opportunely met the challenge of social problems derived from economic liberty. On the other hand, the same democratic socialists and social democrats have earned (although perhaps not deserved) the opprobrium and hatred of the "scientific" socialists, who scorn all democratic considerations and all reformism, and live only for the day when the last property owner will have been hanged with the guts of the last priest.

Marxism

It is in the works of Karl Marx where the socialist critique of capitalism is expressed with maximum force and coherence. Marx fused all previous socialist thought into a powerful synthesis, adding the crucial prophecy of the inevitability of socialism, and assigning to the industrial proletariat the principal role in the solution to the class struggle and the end of history. After Marx, socialism and Marxism have practically been synonyms. Reformists and revisionists almost invariably have wanted no more than to interpret Marx correctly. Only in very recent years have we seen heterodox revisionist currents, and even extravagant assertions that "Marx is dead" on the part of ideologues who call themselves socialist.

Before Marx, socialist thinkers mostly expressed vague and emotional condemnations of capitalist society, showing too clearly the reactionary nucleus of nostalgia for the past characteristic of the socialist spirit. They proposed, if anything, weak and utopian solutions, such as the government of well-intentioned technocrats (Saint-Simon) or communist nodules within capitalist society: the *falansteries* of Fourier, the national workshops of Louis Blanc, Proudhon's mutualism or the cooperative communities of Robert Owen.

Other pre-Marxist socialists were passionate believers in violence and revolutionary terror, but they lacked the historicist alibi, that wonderful all-purpose proposition that history has a rational and predictable development that will absolve those who use violence and terror in favor of the good cause. That lack of justification through historicism exposed Babeuf's Equals and other similar sects clearly for what they really were: outbursts of resentment, anger, and frustration exercising a thirst for revenge on the part of the humiliated of society against the rich and the powerful.

To all of them Marx owes a debt much greater than he ever fully acknowledged. But in contrast with them, he saw the need for theories that would lead to practical action within the actual conditions generated by industrial capitalism. And most important of all, he conceived and formulated a historicism that was powerfully appropriate to the sensitivity of the era.

The class struggle had been a common place of all social critics since the invention of writing, and surely before that as well. Marx formulated the fundamental hypothesis that such conflicts are the movers of history, and that human conflicts are above all differences in economic interests—something that once said seemed obvious and at the same time irrefutable. From these hypotheses he derived a grandiose conclusion: economic relations are and had always been the essence of social organization.

Successive dominant classes have derived their power from having made at some point the decisive contribution to economic affairs of society. This has invariably given rise to a form of social organization in which the greater contributors to production have received, or rather grabbed, the essentials of political and cultural power. This class has developed perceptions and interpretations of the world (its religion, philosophy, ethics, esthetics) that have taken the appearance of universal and immutable truths.

Until now all the dominant classes have based their prosperity on the exploitation of other classes. Only human work can produce wealth. Therefore, the accumulation of capital cannot happen except through the exploitation of man by his fellow man; through theft by some (the minority) of a part of the work of others (invariably the majority). All of human history, since the destruction of a hypothetical primitive communism by the establishment of private property, had been a chronicle of exploitation and iniquities. From the French Revolution on, and conspicuously in the contemporary era (of Marx), the class that had established its political and cultural domination, after having contributed the most to production for a long period before 1789, was the industrial and financial bourgeoisie.

The Virtuous and the Wicked

Since Marx held that he was a scientist discovering the laws of historical development, he should not have permitted himself the luxury of moral reprobation against the bourgeoisie, a class that in conformity with those presumed laws was simply brilliantly performing its predetermined and ineluctable role. But it is obvious that Marx (as all socialists) was moved above all, if not exclusively, by an emotional rejection of liberal capitalist society, before all theory and intellectual speculation.

The persuasive power of Marx resides above all in the eloquence both of his anticapitalist denunciations and of his prophecy, and very secondarily in his pseudoscientific reasoning. This explains the peculiarity that although his so-called laws of historical development and his political economy have been successfully refuted theoretically and (what is more important) factually, the Marxist gospel continues to have a powerful influence and has become in practice a veritable religion.

Other essential aspects of Marx are his genuine indignation against the injustices of capitalist society, lending a biblical grandeur to his writing, and his surprising intellectual arrogance in the conviction that he was totally correct, and that all of his adversaries, including those socialists who were not disposed to bow before his leadership, were totally wrong.

This last feature of Marx touches a sensitive cord in authoritarian characters, as are socialists who seriously seek power and eventually get it. Marx invented a singularly appropriate style for such types: a brutal, aggressive, Jupiterian form of speaking, writing and acting.

Moreover, he fostered the presumption that those who understand where history is heading and dedicate themselves to pushing it along are therefore liberated from ordinary moral ties. In the eternal clash between good and evil, the Marxist, by virtue of simply being one, is on the side of the angels. History becomes a morality play. In any moment of its development, there are virtuous "progressive" forces and individuals and wicked "reactionary" forces and individuals: and at its end, salvation.

And all of this was proposed in a moment when the idea that God was dead (in the phrase of Nietzsche) was in vogue; history appeared empty of content, a story told by an idiot, full of sound and fury, signifying nothing. For some people, Marxism was, and remains, just what was required to fill the gap. This seduction paradoxically has begun to operate belatedly in the heart and guts of some Christians, including priests. This group of recent converts to Marxism apparently no longer feel within themselves any echo of the existence of the God in which they thought they had believed.

The Marxist Ethic

The "new ethic" formulated by Marx and practiced by his disciples was destined to have very serious consequences that even today poison public affairs and many private lives.

It is undeniable that something of the same spirit always existed in human beings and was part of the motivation for the religious wars and for the extermination of heretics by innumerable orthodoxies—that is, the same comfortable and merciless conviction that one is totally correct and that one has the gleeful obligation to stamp out sin and sinners, to chastise error and uproot it by any means, including the greatest coercion, torture and capital punishment.

But, except in times of collective hysteria, witch hunts or pogroms against Jews that went out of control, heresy used to consist of a more or less well-defined deviation with relation to dogmas that were also more or less clearly formulated; it could not be just hurled as an unanswerable accusation against any individual or group, simply because political considerations, cynical or principled, dictated as convenient the destruction of that individual or that group. The classical trials for heresy, or against ideas, as in the cases of Joan of Arc or Galileo (and even the judicial asassination of the Templars by Philippe le Bel) were conducted with reference to criteria understood and in some form accepted as clear and objective by the judges as well as the accused. The victim suffered prison, torture, and death feeling and knowing that he was innocent, and in the certainty that his executioners were either mistaken or acting in bad faith.

The same cannot be said of the profoundly and essentially Marxist (not only Stalinist) Moscow trials, or any of the political trials conducted by the Marxists before the court of history. A Marxist is always right, simply by virtue of being one, against any non-Marxist. And a Marxist in power is always right against a Marxist in opposition. Rubashov-Bukharin is rightly jailed and will be rightly shot not for being less Marxist than Stalin, but because "Number One" is the General Secretary and, as such, Supreme Priest and irrefutable interpreter of the historical dialectic, so that, "objectively" any opposition to his personal power effectively turns into a counterrevolutionary crime.[4]

The power of a Marxist state or the use of Marxist armed force in civil or international wars is not touched by embarrassment on account of scruples; Marxist napalm on a village in Afghanistan will be different from United States napalm on a Vietnamese village. It is true that lately there have been bloody struggles among Marxist states, of Vietnam against Cambodia, of China against Vietnam, without counting the Soviet invasions of Hungary and Czechoslovakia—but in those cases it is only necessary to suspend judgment until history sees the final victor. That side was right; communist force or cunning will always be identical to the highest interest of humanity, which exempts Marxist-Leninist socialists even from the need to behave with common charity and decency in their personal and family affairs.

There is in all of this an unprecedented philosophical justification for the most brutal public and private behavior. This having occurred in our time, under cover of the ideals of socialism, comprises the greatest setback suffered by humanist and progressive hopes conceived of by the enlightenment. The Marxist "new ethic" has resulted not in an advance in the tortuous process of humanization of the "naked monkey," but rather in a catastrophic setback. Marxist reason, if we divest it of its arbitrary historicist justification, reveals itself to be the invariable servant of power, faithful apologist of the police, accomplice of torturers and executioners.

"Don't Make Billancourt Dispair"

If we have understood this, it will no longer surprise us that the use of Marxist ideology as a catechism for the conduct of the government of society even by truly exceptional men such as Lenin, Stalin or Mao

Tse Tung (and all of this within a wide variety of circumstances that today includes previously modern, democratic and industrialized societies such as Czechoslovakia) has produced uniformly deplorable results.

Some communist leaders have come to admit this on the most solemn occasions. It is unlikely that there are still those who reject Nikita Khrushchev's report to the Twentieth Congress of the Communist party of the Soviet Union as apocryphal. Excluding the unlikely event that someone were to still believe the Khrushchev Report to be false and invented by the CIA, today the whole world knows— although the fact is diversely interpreted—that what happened in Russia starting in 1917 is one of the greatest combinations of degradation and suffering that history has recorded. And there is really no logical or ideological gap between what has occured in the Soviet Union, above all under the Stalin tyranny, and the genocide perpetrated by the Cambodian communists against their own people. Up to now, this genocide represents the extreme consequence of forcing, by means of the extermination of "irrecuperable persons" and of terror against the very few survivors, the theoretical Marxist conditions for the rise of the new man, classless society, and communism.

Where regimes dedicated to this inhuman utopia have become stabilized after having assassinated, jailed, exiled, and in general terrorized the population, so that the survivors are submissive, those regimes have had to confront the problem of governing in times of civil and foreign peace.

It then becomes quickly apparent that four-fifths of Marxism's propositions must be abandoned because they are incompatible with social life (for example, the pretense that the monetary economy, buying and selling, or salaries can be abolished) and that the residue, imposed by the greatest coercion, produces societies where the common citizen is virtually always an outlaw. A juridical order inspired in Marxism is contrary to nature and impossible to abide, so that everyone has to get along more or less through subterfuge and petty transgressions. And in practice the state exercises discretional powers, ignores its own laws, and maintains common citizens in a situation of virtual permanent guilt. This is established beyond doubt from countless coinciding testimonies. Even the most stubborn Marxists know it. And if they continue to deny it, it is so as "not to make Billancourt dispair,"[5] as Sartre once cynically put it.

At this stage, sixty-eight years after the Soviet Revolution, when the Soviet Union has long since ceased to be a besieged and threatened entity and has rather become a threatening superpower, what persists in happening there cannot be explained as an accident, anomaly, or deviation, but as a general tendency of socialism. The attempt to reach utopia guided by Marxist maps and the Marxist compass time and again produces monsters. With the abolition of private property and the market economy, the struggle for political power becomes the only field of competition between capable and ambitious individuals. From that struggle will invariably emerge victorious the most brutal, cruel, and unscrupulous, the Stalins. And this will happen all the more swiftly since the leaders of any socialist revolution will have been previously rendered immune, by Marxist historicism and by the Marxist new ethic, to what Marx disqualified as "bourgeois morality." Such abolition of the inhibitions that non-Marxists conserve with respect to the limits that human rights place on coercion and repression, leads in practice to the extermination by the hard-line Marxists (the ones who reach power) of the class enemy and, in passing, of such soft-line Marxists as cannot keep up during or after the process of the consolidation of socialist power.

The theory of the special mission of the proletariat and of the irrecuperability of the class enemy justifies the destruction of all cultural values existing in society before the seizure of power by the Marxists, and also the moral, psychological, and eventually the physical destruction of human beings who hold those values.

In its extreme, this inhuman insanity, this return to the kind of barbarism that preceded the recognition by the higher religions of the dignity of all men, reaches the Cambodian delirium: the systematic extermination of all literate adults to smooth over the obstacles for the arrival of the new man. And this satanic genocide took place only yesterday, which proves that with the passing of time Marxism, instead of losing virulence, accumulates it, since its faithful tend to attribute the previous failures of their pseudoreligion to lack of fervor, devotion and human sacrifices.

Political Development Is a Precondition of Economic and Social Development

The fundamental change effected by the Marxist socialist revolutions is none other than the abolition of private property and the resulting state ownership of the means of production. What immediately has happened where socialism has triumphed has to be credited or charged to the immense consequences of such major surgical intervention undergone by an organism—human society—which at all times and under all circumstances, except some eccentric (not to say, aberrant) deviations[6], has functioned on the basis of some form of private property.

Under conditions of general insecurity, close to anarchy, or, inversely, when society has been crushed by arbitrary and discretionary power, private property has been precarious, and for that reason, of little social value. Advances in civil peace that diminish the likelihood that property rights can be defied by force, and the rule of law that finally makes them secure, are developments that should be regarded as clear and net gains for all society (not only for property owners) and as having been crucial to the progress of civilization and human freedom and dignity. Where the rights of property owners have been recognized, respected, and protected, this has invariably meant a retreat of the discretionary and brutal use of political power. The triumph of the bourgeois revolution against absolutism was the culmination of that advance, and introduced to the West a political and juridical order conducive to the colossal development of productive forces implicit in the industrial revolution. That revolution consumated the legitimacy of private property and its protection under law, not only vis-à-vis the challenge of other private persons who would use violence to despoil a property owner, but most important vis-à-vis arbitrary political power, and such extortions, whimsical and exorbitant taxes and confiscations as political power had previously been able to impose on industry and commerce.

It was an immense political revolution that which assigned to the state the duty of protecting and facilitating commercial transactions among private persons instead of impeding them, imposing oppressive rates, confiscating, causing humiliation, and generating insecurity. Starting then the world would witness the apparently inexplicable miracle of that explosion of economic growth to which Marx and Engels refer with amazement in the *Communist Manifesto.* And an even more surprising miracle would occur: the correlative rise of freedoms, political rights, and the dignity of all human beings, for the first time recognized not as eccentric concerns of sensitive souls, but rather as natural rights, requiring obligatory recognition by governments. On top of that, an attitude change would extend to ever larger circles of the class of property owners that, if still not solidly held, at least broke through indifference toward non–property owners and the weakest members of society. This last was a revolution in feelings and attitudes that is still going on in the capitalist societies. It is a revolution that is manifested in the rise of socialist thought, but that is not exclusive to the socialists, existing in the conscience of all who have been touched by the liberal humanist world view. It lies, for example, at the foundation of the guilt feelings of the developed world about the poverty and backwardness of the Third World.

From Socialism to the Third World Ideology

The ideological power of Marxist historicism and salvationism and its capacity to satisfy emotions is perhaps invulnerable to reasoning based on facts. Everywhere, all who are discontented or uneasy with themselves or with their state in the world, tend to accept the general assumptions and propositions of that historicist salvationism with its pantheon of gods and its gallery of demons. In particular, the sham axiom is accepted that capitalism and the resulting westernization of the world in the last two-hundred years are at the origin of all evils. The final salvation of humanity, then, will dawn with the defeat and extinction of a devil named "Imperialism," embodied in a certain number of advanced capitalist countries, whose weakening and eventual destruction will be the equivalent to the battle of Armageddon, the last Judgement, when the just will ascend to the heaven of communism and the wicked will be thrown into the dustbin of history.

Thus we are confronted with the paradox that even though Marxist-Leninist socialism has proved repulsive to the advanced industrial societies where supposedly it should have easily triumphed, its spread, starting from the power base that is the Soviet Union, has taken place mostly in the backward countries. Its spread to these countries is characterized by formal adherence to the Marxist-Leninist orthodoxy, and by shades of "nonalignment" basically accepting the proposition that western democracies are essentially and hopelessly adversaries of progress and the welfare of the other countries of the earth, while the Soviet Union is the friend and natural ally of the so-called Third World.

This perversion of nonalignment and the resulting effect of making ever larger areas of the Third World cannon fodder for the benefit of the Soviet superpower, are currently the most ambiguous and unhealthy components of the socialist spirit. Almost all socialists—not only the Marxist-Leninists but also the democratic socialists and even the social democrats—are infected by the fixed idea that the advance of socialism can and must occur from now on in the poor and backward countries, which should replace the "corrupted" proletariat of the West as the essential carrier of world socialism. Only in this way can we explain that both the democratic socialists and social democrats should not object to, but rather celebrate in the Soviets' and their Cuban surrogates' confiscation of the Nicaraguan revolution.

This attitude and the body of ideas, beliefs, and emotions that underlie it are what I call the Third World ideology. It does not seem to matter that it should be at once confused and simplistic; instead, this seems to be an essential part of its appeal. And clearly it has become the most vital and most widely shared current component of the socialist spirit, serving it as compensation for the failures and disappointments of socialism so far.

This is a situation that would have surprised the original socialists. Marx and Engels, especially, would have rejected as barbaric and full of danger the proposition that there is a predestined affinity between socialism and underdevelopment.[7]

Notes

1. In an article entitled "Individualism and Socialism," *Revue Encyclopédique,* Paris, 1833.
2. Ibid.
3. Ibid.
4. Bukharin was the model for Rubashov, the hero of Arthur Koestler's *Darkness at Noon.*
5. Jean-Paul Sartre thought that Khrushchev's revelations against Stalin in the Twentieth Congress of the Soviet Communist Party were an "enormous mistake," and even "madness." He declared to the French magazine *L'Express* (19 November 1956): [In this matter of "destalinization"] "one ought to have known what it was one wanted, and how far one wanted to go, undertake reforms without shouting about them from the rooftops. . . . In my opinion, the Khrushchev revelations have been an enormous mistake. One can't go on and expose in detail the crimes of a sacred figure [Stalin] who embodied the regime for so long. . . . The result has been shocking to masses who were not yet ready for the truth. When one sees how this has affected intellectuals here in France, one can measure how, say, the Hungarian workers were unprepared to understand this terrible relation of crimes revealed without explanation, without analysis, without prudence."
6. For example, the anarcho-communist regime imposed in the first third of the sixteenth century in various towns in Bohemia by the taborists; or the communist terror that afflicted Münster under Juan Matthys and Jan Bockelson (Jan de Leyden) in 1534-35. This second episode is particularly illustrative. Matthys and Bockelson seized Münster as Anabaptist preachers. On February 23, 1534, they achieved a majority in the town council, and a litte later they established an implacable theocratic dictatorship. Lutherans and Catholics who still had not escaped from Münster were assassinated, expelled or converted by force. By 3 March, Münster had been purged of all evil and was ready to live in mutual love, perfect equality and disinterestedness. Matthys took advantage of the necessity to organize the defense of the city in order to abolish private property. A blacksmith dared to object. Matthys had him arrested and demanded his execution before the townfolk, gathered together for the occasion in the market place. Some other craftsmen and merchants who protested the arbitrariness of the

procedure were arrested as well. Matthys in person executed the dissident blacksmith. From then on terror was unleashed. Matthys proclaimed that true Christians must not own anything, and that all money and all valuable objects should be given to the town government. Those who resisted were executed. At the end of two months, the monetary economy had ceased to exist in Münster. The following step was the institution of common property of all goods, including houses and food. Communal dining halls were established. Everything belonged to everyone. There must no longer be "Mine" and "Thine." The following is from a pamphlet published in Münster in October 1534: "Everything which has served the purpose of selfseeking and private property, such as buying and selling, working for money, taking interest and practising usury . . . or eating and drinking the sweat of the poor . . . all such things are abolished amongst us by the power of love and community." Matthys and Bockelson moreover decreed a "cultural revolution." When in the first days they plundered the cathedral, they were specially intent on the books and manuscripts of the library. In March, Matthys prohibited all books except the Bible. All other books were brought to the cathedral square and burned in a huge bonfire, to break with the past and to protect the inhabitants of Münster from contamination with ideas contrary to those that they should now exclusively have. Convinced of his invulnerability, Matthys led an attack against the besiegers and was killed. The Stalin of that Lenin was Jan Bockelson, who swiftly destroyed the pretense of collegiate power that Matthys had maintained in the form of the town council. Bockelson proclaimed himself as Supreme Judge, with absolute authority in all public and private, spiritual and material matters, as well as with power of life and death over all citizens. Guilds were dissolved. Craftsmen were turned into government employees, without salary. Bockelson proclaimed a new penal code in which all acts of "insubordination" were punishable by death, first against God and his representative in Münster, Jan Bockelson, but also of a child against his parents or a wife against her husband, etc. Sexual transgressions were also punished; this last had an unexpected turn when Bockelson decided to establish polygamy. In a few weeks he himself took fifteen wives. Women who refused to share their husband or to marry men already married were tortured and executed. Fights among the wives of a man also resulted in punishment by death. In August 1534, Bockelson proclaimed himself King. From then on he abandoned all pretense of poverty and humbleness, lived in luxury and pomp, dressed in splendid clothing, crowned in gold and surrounded by a numerous court. His favorite wife was crowned queen. In contrast with the luxury and abundance of the court, the people of Münster were by then in utter destitution, because in the name of equality and disinterestedness everything had been taken from them except the clothing they wore. With the confiscated horses, Bockelson formed a Praetorian mounted guard that surrounded him in his outings in the street. By January 1535 Münster was exhausted and continued under siege. While hunger devastated the city, the court of Bockelson, it was discovered, had hoarded so much food that at the end the King, his wives, his courtesans, and guards still had provisions for another six months. Bockelson would have resisted those six months, and all of Münster would have perished by starvation while the court continued eating and drinking. But two desperate citizens opened the city to the besiegers on the night of July 24 1535. See Norman Cohn, *The Pursuit of the Millennium* (London: Secker & Warburg Ltd., 1957).

7. One can surmise what Marx and Engels would have thought of the Third World ideology, from the following quotation from Engels' *On Social Relations in Russia* (1875):

> The revolution which modern Socialism strives to achieve is, briefly, the victory of the proletariat over the bourgeoisie, and the establishment of a new organization of society by the destruction of all class distinctions. This requires not only a proletariat that carries out this revolution, but also a bourgeoisie in whose hands the productive forces of society have developed so far that they allow of the final destruction of class distinctions.

> Only at a certain level of development of the productive forces of society, an even very high level of our modern conditions, does it become possible to raise production to such an extent that the abolition of class distinctions can be a real progress, can be lasting without bringing about stagnation or even decline in the mode of social production. But the productive forces have reached this level of development only in the hands of the bourgeoisie. The bourgeoisie, therefore, in this respect also is just as necessary a precondition of the socialist revolution as the proletariat itself. Hence a man who will say that this revolution can be more easily carried out in a country, because, although it has no proletariat, it has no bourgeoisie either, only proves that he has still to learn the ABC of Socialism.

Equally relevant is the following quotation from Marx's *Preface to the Critique of Political Economy:*

> No social order ever perishes before all the productive forces for which there is room in it have developed; and new, higher relations of production never appear before the material conditions of their existence have matured in the womb of the old society itself. Therefore mankind always sets itself only such tasks as it can solve; since, looking at the matter more closely, it will always be found that the task itself arises only when the material conditions for its solution already exist or are at least in the process of formation. (See Karl Marx and Frederick Engels, *Selected Works,* 2 vols. (Moscow: Foreign Language Publishing House, 1947).

3

What Is the Third World?

The term "Third World" came up during the cold war. It implied the existence, after 1945, of states or nations which, without being entirely unscathed by it, could at least remain uninvolved in the struggle between the West, led by the United States, and the Communist Bloc, under the hegemony of the Soviet Union. But insofar as that was meant, the term "Third World" was misleading. While it is true that the rivalry between the superpowers and their direct allies has allowed some countries to play the game called "neutralism" or "nonalignment," very few countries included in what has been since called the "Third World" had any real possibility of remaining neutral. The majority of them were then members of the coalition led by the United States. Many had not yet gained their national independence. Western influence—North American or European—was dominant in others that had long been independent, such as those in Latin America, or in those that had never been colonies, such as Afghanistan or Thailand. China was, under the government of Chiang Kai Shek, an ally of the West.

Thirty-five years later the situation has been astonishingly reversed. The so-called Third World is increasingly distancing itself from the West and, moreover, adopting positions favorable to the Soviet Union, an evolution that has accelerated in the last years with the bold military and diplomatic Soviet expansion in Africa and around the Persian Gulf, and through Afghanistan toward the Indian Ocean. Latin America is experiencing the second wave of the ideological and military expansionism of the Cuban Revolution, as different from the romantic and disorganized adventure of Che Guevara in Bolivia as is the Cuban expedition to Angola from Che's futile attempt to stir up revolution in the Congo in the early sixties. China's farsighted anxiety about this trend led to a rapprochement with the West, a development that could create conditions that would slow down Soviet advances in the Third World, in some cases checking them and even rolling them back. But this belongs to the domain of speculation, while the hard fact is that, since 1945, the Soviet Union has gained great strategic advantage against the West in the territories now called the Third World.

Why and how has this happened? Why has the Third World become so antagonistic to the West and at the same time so open to Soviet influence and subversion, directly or through surrogates such as Cuba or Vietnam?

The International Social Question

The birth and development of the Third World question shows a remarkable analogy to the rise and the development of the social question starting from the Industrial Revolution. Both phenomena are similar in their causes—in the emotions they stir and feed upon, in their panoply of ideas and categories, and even in the vocabulary used to offer supposed solutions to situations perceived as intolerable. There are also differences, but they have been glossed over in the successful attempt to apply to international relations the categories used in the nineteenth century to describe, explain, and propose remedies to class relations within capitalist industrial society. The most fundamental difference is that relations between the advanced capitalist nations and the underdeveloped African, Asiatic or marginal Western (Latin American) nations are external, a rubbing of surfaces; while the relations between social classes within industrial society were in the nineteenth century (and remain today) an internal problem of each nation, and can therefore be submerged by or relegated most of the time to nationalism.

But the analogies exist, and have permitted an interpretation of the relations between the "First" and the Third Worlds which is an analogue of the Marxist theory of the class struggle between the bourgeoisie and the proletariat. This struggle, according to Marxism, should have led to revolution and socialism in the advanced capitalist countries. Since that Marxist prophecy was not fulfilled, what I call the Third World ideology came to the rescue, substituting the failed prophecy with a similar and vaster drama: the struggle between "proletarian" and "bourgeois" nations.

The English Marxist John Atkinson Hobson first gave this new twist to the topic of the struggle between the rich and the poor as the driving force of history and ferment of revolution. Hobson put forward his ideas in a book aptly called *Imperialism* (1902), which is the source of Lenin's far better known *Imperialism, the Supreme Stage of Capitalism* (1916), a pamphlet crucial to the Third World ideology. Here are some characteristic quotations from that Leninist tract:

Capitalism has created a handful (fewer than a tenth of the inhabitants of the earth) of rich and powerful States that plunder the rest of the world.

Obviously, starting from such gigantic super-profits (obtained over and above from the profits that the capitalists wrest from the workers in their own countries) it is possible to *bribe* the trade union leaders and the whole super-stratum of the labor aristocracy . . . a sector of the working class which the capitalists thus manage to "bourgoisify" . . . to make them agents of the bourgeoisie in the heart of the working class.

We will not advance a milimeter toward the solution of the practical problems of the communist movement and the revolution until we understand this phenomenon and we appreciate its political and sociological meaning.

The division of the world into two groups, the colonialist countries, on the one hand, and the colonized countries on the other, is not the only characteristic (of Imperialism). There also are *dependent* countries: countries that officially enjoy political independence, but in fact are entangled in the (imperialist) system of economic and diplomatic dependence.

(Imperialism) is a form of parasitic and rotten capitalism (a vulnerable system because) its circumstances in all the countries involved determine the sociopolitical conditions (favorable to the revolution).[1]

The Ingredients of the Third World Ideology

Having seized the nerve centers of the czarist empire, the Bolsheviks immediately gave first priority to those assymetrical relations of the advanced capitalist countries with their colonies. They could serve as a base for communist-inspired nationalist agitation in the backyard of the colonial powers, and in this way alleviate the pressure that those powers were exerting against the final establishment of bolshevism in Russia. Lenin and his followers shrewdly perceived what I described as the "international social question" and its potential virulence. Just how shrewd and to the point were the Bolsheviks' insight becomes apparent by reading their *Thesis on the Colonial and National Question* (stated in the Second Congress of the Communist International, Moscow 1920). Reading these theses is essential if one is to understand the history of the last sixty-five years, particularly for the correct interpretation of the years from 1945, when decolonization and revolution swept the territories today known as the Third World.

The theses state that the allegedly equal relations between sovereign nations in fact cover up the enslavement of the great majority of the world's population by a very limited minority—the bourgeoisie and the workers' aristocracy of the advanced capitalist countries—and that it will be impossible to abolish this slavery and to eliminate inequalities between the rich and the poor countries without first destroying capitalism throughout the world.

Once this is understood, the theses then argue, the political evolution and history of the world will be seen to revolve around the struggle between the advanced, capitalist, imperialist countries and the revolutionary Soviet power. In order to survive and to win, the Soviet Union will have to enroll the support of all the "proletarian vanguard groups" of the world (that is to say, all the parties affiliated, or ready to be affiliated, with the Communist International), as well as all the nationalist movements in the colonial territories and dependent countries. These nationalist movements will have to be persuaded that their interests and aspirations converge (and are in fact identical) with the defense and promotion of Soviet power, and thus with the progress and future triumph of world revolution.

The Communist parties, therefore, will have to follow a policy of "realizing the closest possible union between all national and colonial liberation movements and Soviet Russia;" the form of this alliance in each separate colony or dependent country will be determined by the stage of development that its Communist movement and its corresponding national liberation movements will have reached.

> It [will be] necessary . . . to explain constantly that only the Soviet regime is able to give the nations real equality [and likewise] to support the revolutionary movement among the subject nations, [for example] Ireland, the American Negroes. . . . The victory over capitalism cannot be fully achieved and carried to its ultimate goals unless the proletariat [of the advanced capitalist countries] and the toiling masses [of colonial and dependent countries] rally . . . in a heartfelt and close union. . . . One of the main sources from which . . . capitalism draws its chief strength is to be found in the colonial possessions and dependencies. Without the control of those extensive markets and vast fields of exploitation, capitalism cannot maintain its existence even for a short time. . . . Extra profits gained in the colonies and dependent countries are the mainstay of modern capitalism, and

so long as the latter is not deprived of this source of extra profit it will not be easy for . . . the working class [i.e., the Communist parties of the advanced capitalist countries] to overthrow the capitalist order. . . . Thus, it is the breaking up of the colonial empire [and the emancipation of the dependent countries] together with the [then inevitable] proletarian revolution in each home country that will overthrow the capitalist system in advanced capitalist countries. . . . In order to promote these objectives, it must be taken into account that there are to be found in the dependent countries [and in the colonies] two distinct movements. . . . One is the bourgeois democratic nationalist movement, and the other is the mass action of the poor and ignorant peasants and workers for their liberation from all forms of exploitation. . . . The cooperation of the bourgeois nationalist revolutionary elements is useful for the overthrow of foreign imperialistic capitalism, which is the first step toward socialist revolution in the colonies [and dependent countries]. . . . Thus the masses in the backward countries may reach Communism, not through capitalist development, but directly under the leadership of the class-conscious proletariat of the advanced capitalist countries [i.e., the Third International].[2]

These theories were later to acquire more subtle and veiled formulations, while they imposed themselves throughout the world; in a sense, whenever anyone uses the expression "Third World," he is tacitly endorsing some of the basic assumptions contained in the "Theses of the Third International," formulated in its 1920 Congress in Moscow.

This does not mean of course that the events, almost uniformly adverse to the West, that have occurred in recent years in Cuba, Africa, North Yemen, Iran, Southeast Asia, Afghanistan, and Central America have been shaped solely by agitation spurred by the Soviet Union; the seed existed before the Third World ideology was formulated and became a guideline for the international communist movement. But in retrospect it is remarkable how Lenin and his Bolshevik companions early and perfectly realized the explosive force of subterranean discontent in Africa, Asia and Latin America, as a consequence of the economic, political and cultural domination of the West. Even more surprising is the mobilizing power of that antiwestern alienation and hostility in the very heart of the Western societies.

Whatever its disguises, the Third World ideology consists essentially in the proposition that both the backwardness of the underdeveloped countries and the advance of the advanced capitalist countries are due to colonialism, imperialist exploitation and the ennervating effect of dependence, and notably in the use of that proposition as an open or implicit argument in favor of socialism. Thus it becomes clear why the Third World ideology has become the passion of all those who harbor anticapitalist ideas and feelings not only in the countries classified as Third World, but also, maybe more so, in the advanced capitalist countries themselves.

The anticapitalists are not only communists, or only Marxists, or only socialists (although obviously all these groups, each of which includes the preceding one, have an invincible prejudice against capitalist civilization) but include the dissatisfied, the frustrated, the disoriented, the unfortunate and the irrational within capitalist civilization itself. Anticapitalism also sways those who (like some Christians), although not wholly irrational, fear the rationalist and secularizing implications of capitalism; and also those who, for whatever reason, reject or fear the consequences of scientific and technological development, of industrialism, and the growth of cities.

For members of such a formidable coalition, the so-called Third World appears not as a diversity of nations with varied levels of development and widely different cultures, but as an undifferentiated mass of people and territories; and their essential determination would supposedly be that they are not irrevocably contaminated by capitalist civilization, and are therefore potential recruits in the mounting crusade whose ultimate aim is the destruction of the West.

From the premise that there is an intractable historical conflict between the West and the Third World thus defined, there is but one step to the conclusion that the countries of the Third World have a natural coincidence of interests with the Soviet Union.

What Is the Third World?

The truth of the matter is that the countries today included in the Third World have many more divergences than similarities. They have an extraordinary diversity in their history, culture, demography, climate, geography; and a great variation in capacities, attitudes, customs, living standards, levels of backwardness or of modernization. Included in the Third World are areas of relative stagnation next to others undergoing swift change and even rapid economic advance and accelerated modernization; homogeneous nations and states composed of a mosaic of nations speaking different languages; secularized societies together with others of virulent religious fanaticism; regions with oppressive demographic density and vast almost unpopulated areas;

rigidly stratified societies as if these were comparable to others with great social mobility; inhabitants of modern societies as if they were not differentiated except superficially from aborigines still living in the stone age.

In addition, it is evident that the reason for including such a diversity under a single label is neither poverty nor underdevelopment, because those conditions existed, even worse, before the rise of the Third World ideology. And if poverty and backwardness were sufficient to classify a country as belonging to the Third World, it would be necessary to include states that proclaim themselves to be socialist, but where those conditions exist. Why Argentina, Malaysia and Senegal, and not Cuba, Cambodia or Ethiopia? These latter countries, by what must be unmasked as ideological legerdemain, are supposedly no longer Third World since they ended their imperialism-related "dependence."

A country that enters the Soviet orbit, directly or through actions of Soviet surrogates such as Cuba and Vietnam, not only abolishes thenceforth the free competition between citizens and all participation of civil society in decision making, but is also instantly seen as removed from that universal and documented competition between sovereign states that permits discerning (approximately) the real value of different societies and systems. To be of any meaning, this competition requires the compilation and open publication of reliable statistics, and that vitally important ingredient: the freedom of human beings to choose to remain where they are or to emigrate to escape oppression and seek better opportunities. The Third World syndrome is admitted and proclaimed wherever these conditions more or less persist. But a nation that was yesterday Third World, as soon as it becomes a Soviet Satellite, is as if by miracle transferred by the Third World ideology to a special limbo. Its inhabitants from one day to the next are supposedly exempt from poverty and all other deprivations that afflicted them when their country was affiliated to the world capitalist economic system. The numerous and strident apostles of the Third World ideology will therefore banish countries newly captured by communism from the range of their anguished and obsessive preoccupation with the inequalities among nations. We continue to see them sleepless and tearful about the fate of the Argentinians, Malaysians or Senegalese, while—if we are going to believe them—they rejoice at the sudden happiness that befell the Cubans, the Ethiopians and the Cambodians, and even at the still uncertain bliss of the people of Afghanistan.

Thus, only countries in Asia, Africa and Latin America that are not yet under Soviet domination belong to the Third World. What do they have in common? I would advance the argument that, though very different from one another, they share similar feelings of alienation and antagonism with respect to the successful capitalist countries. To be Third World is to perceive one's position in the world as somewhat like the situation of the colored populations in societies where power is cornered by the whites. In contrast, a New Zealander, a Belgian, an Australian, or a Norwegian does not feel decisively alienated or resentful with regard to bigger, more powerful and richer members of the society of which they form a part (the society of the capitalist nations). And therefore they do not suffer from any obsessive contradiction between emulation and rejection of the values, attitudes and customs of the "whites" of world society. The satisfaction of countries such as New Zealand, Belgium, Australia or Norway with their situations, even though inferior in the world such as it is, is not only due to the fact that their economies work reasonably well and their political institutions are civilized and stable. It is also, and perhaps above all, due to the fact that they feel themselves to be members of the "club" that we call the West. They—and others like themselves—do not feel that their dependence with relation to the most rich and powerful member of the club (once France, then Great Britain, now the United States) is an unbearable distortion of fundamental identity: without stopping to think about it, they include Locke and Descartes among their philosophers; Mozart and Berlioz among their musicians; Shakespeare and Shaw among their playwrights; Dante and Goethe among their poets; and Roosevelt and Churchill among their statesmen.

The question might arise, then, whether Japan should be considered Third World. The answer might be yes, in a certain way, in spite of its emulation of Western industrial and administrative technologies, its assimilation of certain Western values and of the resulting economic success. But does this make Japan a "member of the club?" Surely Japan does not feel as comfortable within world society as does Australia, an infinitely less important country but which is culturally aligned with the West. There has not been and there will not be an Australian Yukio Mishima.

Now, in a world system almost completely built on Western ideas, values and power and more specifically on the hegemony of the Anglo-Saxons—first the English and more recently the Americans—and in an era when the nationalist passion, invented in the West, has assumed a decisive importance, the slightest flaw in identification with the original source of those ideas and values must cause anxiety, insecurity, and dissatisfaction of individuals and nations. At the center of the system those feelings will not be absent because they are universal, but they will be minimal, so that the functioning of society will be smoother, the formulation of goals clearer, and their fulfillment less difficult. Good economic performance will be more probable, and even a modest national product will be equitably distributed rather than grabbed by the holders of political power and their friends. Given these conditions, moderate economic success is sufficient for a society in order to achieve more or less stable equilibrium, which is the characteristic of nonrevolutionary societies.

But as one moves away from the center of the system, anxiety, insecurity, and dissatisfaction will increase, until they become so costly socially that they will end by destroying in these unfortunate "aliens" everything that was in agreement with their own world view and their objective material condition. This is the fundamental cause of unrest in the Third World: an ambivalent, almost schizophrenic attitude with relation to one's own culture, and particularly toward the basic cultural instrument that is language. From such a situation will grow painful feelings of inferiority, self-depreciation, self-hatred, and resulting despair.

These reflections permit us to reach a definition of the Third World that perhaps will be acceptable to those who adhere to the Third World ideology as well as to those who reject it: are Third World those countries that lack confidence in their abilities and possibilities for development within the world capitalist system, inclining them to accept loosely or rigidly the Leninist-Hobsonian thesis on imperialism and dependence to explain their problems. Are Third World those countries which therefore could be induced to disaffiliate themselves in greater or lesser degree from the world capitalist system, and to become, to a corresponding degree, clients of the socialist system and its hegemonic power, the Soviet Union. Such countries can become nonaligned, on a scale from true nonalignment to positions that can lead to submission to the Soviet Union, as in the case of Cuba. This latter situation irrevocably and brutally puts an end to the nuances, ambiguities, vacillations and contradictions characterizing the peculiar restlessness of the Third World.

This is why Cuba and Ethiopia are not included in the Third World, even though their per capita income levels and other indicators of the welfare of the population are inferior—even abysmally inferior—to those of many countries that are still classified as Third World and continue themselves to accept that classification. Thus Argentina, for example, is included as and accepts itself as Third World, but not Italy. Of the latter it would be clearly foolish to state that its social, economic, cultural, and political problems are due to

Western imperialism. Italy, therefore, is called imperialist and Argentina, Third World.[3]

The Case of Latin America

Within this context, Latin America deserves special attention. First, it is a peculiar parcel of the Third World, since from a certain angle it is at least as Western as Canada; but its cultural affiliation with Europe was by way of Spain and Portugal, both foreign to the original capitalist "club" and the corresponding ethic. Second, it is difficult for Latin Americans to psychologically reconcile their evident similarities to the United States with the far different course of their historical development.[4] As a consequence, Latin Americans have allowed themselves to be seduced by the Third World ideology, and today passively or enthusiastically accept being classified as a part of the Third World.

As a region that has been subjected to the overwhelming imperial influence of the United States, Latin America was destined to become fertile ground for cultivation of the Third World ideology in spite of its Western culture. Latin American resentment, partly justified, toward the United States is the main reason that the occurrences in Cuba starting in 1959 so profoundly moved Latin Americans and continue to motivate them. And to some degree, Latin American judgment has, as a result, been clouded both with regard to its own problems and to the true meaning of the planetary confrontation between the Soviet Union and the United States. The political ground of Latin American society has not yet recovered from the earthquake that was the Cuban Revolution. Moreover, there is no possible restoration. What has happened in Cuba starting from 1959 marks the end of an era, at least as much as the Wars of Independence at the beginning of the nineteenth century and their corollary in the form of the Monroe Doctrine of 1828.

During the intervening period of about one hundred and thirty years, Latin America turned into a mosaic of weak and internally troubled sovereign states and lived in a kind of infantilism vis-à-vis the complexities of international politics. Only Simón Bolívar and a few other statesmen of his generation had a direct perception of the diversity of imperialisms, and of the risks that are the lot of the weak and the small in a world in which essential matters are settled by raw power. That handful of lucid and atypical men, born under the Spanish Empire, felt that they were directly involved in the affairs of Europe. At times very closely, they had followed and even lived through events taking place in the great international arena (the cases of Miranda and Bolívar). They had felt the universal fascination aroused by the prodigious adventure of France between 1789 and 1815; they had been able to understand what constitutes strategic power (above all naval power in that era), decisive in the final outcome favorable to England. With this latter country they had maintained assiduous contacts, at times at the highest level, contacts favored by the interest that Whitehall early had in the dissolution of the Spanish Empire in America. After the final fall of Napoleon, those men immediately also perceived the danger of a restoration of the *ancien régime* in America, and for that reason enthusiastically welcomed the Monroe Doctrine. Only Bolívar seems to have understood that from then on Latin America had exchanged the "open" risk of conquest or colonization by one or other of the great European powers for the de facto status of United States protectorate.

The only important breach in that security guaranteed by an imperial hemispheric protector against the greed of nineteenth century European powers was the French expedition in support of the Austrian Prince Maximilian, installed by Napoleon III on the throne of Mexico at a time when Americans were too absorbed in their Civil War to be able to stop this violation of the Monroe Doctrine. But that was the exception to the rule, and the ruling classes of Latin American society became oblivious to the fact that permanent risks exist, in the world as it is, to the security and sovereignty of weak countries. The Monroe Doctrine ended by becoming part of the landscape before their eyes, so that almost no one perceived it as a reduction of sovereignty and an encouragement to irresponsibility. I personally believe that therein lies the truly profound and perhaps irreparable damage that the United States has caused Latin America, and not in the list of grievances that are usually covered by the curse word "imperialism." Political maturity of societies and the realism indispensable for a reasonably efficient national leadership are based on the perception of the precarious character of all security. A society that aspires to endure and survive in a hostile environment must exert itself at every moment. It must realize that its margin of security will correspond to the good or bad administration of its own resources. It must develop an adequate and efficient military force (not a musical comedy army) and design and carry out consistently a realistic and intelligent foreign policy. A society that meets those minimum conditions of external security will probably find that it has therefore also found the road to modernization and economic development, which are more the consequence than the cause of political maturity.

The Falkland Islands War

Argentina's way of starting and conducting the Falkland War was a conpendium of the attitudes and conduct that have until now retarded that indispensable political maturity in Latin American societies, and even set them back from levels previously reached. Of this last misfortune, Argentina is the most important and saddest example. In the third or fourth week of the Falkland crisis, James Reston wrote in the *New York Times* that the Argentinian generals had already won, but seemed not to have realized it. Any ceasefire at that point, and even more so after the cruel sinking by the English of the Argentinian cruiser *Belgrano,* would have decisively advanced Buenos Aires' goal of sovereignty over the islands. At about the same time, Henry Kissinger said publicly that the Falklands would be under Argentinian sovereignty within the next three years. The Peruvian proposition of a ceasefire, in principle accepted by Great Britain, followed by a provisional administration by four Latin American nations representing the United Nations, was a wide and open avenue toward that outcome. The only doubtful issue at that time seemed to be whether the Georgian and the South Sandwich islands—much farther away than and quite distinct from the Falklands—would remain under British sovereignty, and under what conditions.

In this light it seems incomprehensible that the military *junta* in Buenos Aires multiplied its objections and obstacles to the ceasefire, insisting, for example, that the British fleet first withdraw to its bases in Great Britain. And Buenos Aires did not speak with a single voice, never clarifying whether Argentina had become at least flexible about the impossible precondition for the ceasefire that somehow the British should promise an eventual transfer of sovereignty, which was precisely the question to be negotiated. The fighting thus became inevitable and a painful and humiliating military defeat for Argentina instead of the diplomatic victory that had been within its grasp, which would have been achieved if its rulers had only known where to stop. Latin America reacted to this catastrophic outcome in typically Third World fashion, blaming others for its own mistakes: the English were blamed for their intransigence (which was less than is said) and for their remorseless way of making war, as if it were a game; the Americans, for not having taken Argentina's side, when a halfway-serious political analysis (evidently absent from the initial Argentinian decision) would have foreseen United States neutrality as the most reasonable expectation for Argentina; the UN Security Council, conveniently forgetting that the Soviet Union and China did not veto Resolution 502, which, in demanding the withdrawal of Argentinian troops, showed that the communist powers also considered it vital that territorial disputes should not be settled by force; and its own Organization of American States (OAS) for its irresolution, although it is the only international assembly in which a great power, the greatest of all, takes a seat as an equal, without having the right to veto, so that if a common mind had really existed among the Latin American Governments, the resolutions of the Conference of Ministers of the OAS could have been as strong as Latin America had wished. And if they were not, but rather lukewarm and ambiguous, it was because without openly saying so, the majority of Latin American governments secretly shared the same reservations and objections to Argentinian behavior that publicly they pretended to repudiate.

Latin America, having been deprived by Monroism of an environment of natural selection in which political maturity would have been the condition for survival, suffered instead a regression toward the muddled thinking and the irresponsibility that the creole upper class was accustomed to before the North American and French revolutions produced the "odd" generation of independence. The brew of Monroism and the political, economic and cultural legacy of three centuries of Spanish Empire produced after 1830 a generalized mediocrity, and especially that political underdevelopment, explained by Jean François Revel,[5] in which lies the deepest explanation for the frustrations of a society that deserves better.

Latin America's predominantly Western character should be conducive to modernization, economic and social development, and the stable functioning of democracy. Some of these countries had great cities and modern institutions such as universities well before the United States. The region possesses, moreover, exceptional advantages in its rich variety of natural resources: minerals; arable land; ample space in relation to the population; varied and frequently mild climates; and vast navigable river systems constituting a volume of fresh water unequalled anywhere else and enormous hydroelectric potential. In all, these are important relative advantages that clearly set Latin America apart from the rest of the so-called Third World.

After 1945, when the interamerican system reached its peak and the United States enjoyed not only hemispheric but world hegemony, the guaranteed and "freeload" security of Latin America reached the point that even wars between Latin American states were no longer conceivable. In any case they were stoppable in a few hours through the machinery of the interamerican system, such as in the so-called Football war between Honduras and El Salvador in 1969. In the new era inaugurated by the Cuban revolution and coinciding with the generalized erosion of American power in the world, it is not fortuitous if important wars have again become possible in Latin America, as in the one that more than once was at the point of breaking out between

Argentina and Chile over the Beagle Canal. Also, long and bloody civil wars have taken place, like the one in Nicaragua, with its duplicate being attempted in El Salvador; and to all of this, the United States can react only with extreme caution.

With this crisis in Monroism, denied by Washington for many years but later officially recognized even in presidential speeches,[6] Latin American leaders have discovered with some anguish the basic precariousness of their states, as much in their internal structures as, sometimes, in their very existence. It should be evident that the alibi according to which all the disagreeable things that happen in Latin America are due to foreign agents (United States imperialism or—the reverse side of the same counterfeit coin—the international communist conspiracy) has failed. Latin America must be the last region of the globe where educated people with access to all of the information continue to believe (or pretend to) that the Americans are omniscient and all powerful. Jean-François Revel quotes Leopoldo Zea's surprising dialectic, according to which the old complicity of Washington with the dictators of Latin America was a manifestation of Yankee imperialism (which is a truism), but the pressure of the Carter administration against the dictatorships of the right was also a diabolical form of neoimperialism. Supposedly the United States is so astute and powerful that it can do anything, Latin America nothing. Even in the case of the Cuban Revolution, whose prestige and enormous importance are totally due to the fact that it was the first serious reverse suffered by American hegemony in the hemisphere, its sad failure, after twenty-five years of sacrifice of the Cuban people, will be explained away by the evil doings of the United States.

In this way, paranoia continues to keep a number of Latin American leaders in politics and economics at the level of the most backward and worst informed of the recently decolonized and truly poor countries.

The Example of Japan

A way of at least partially overcoming the Third World neurosis is for a country to achieve unquestionable success in the areas of modernization and economic development, the same areas to which the West owes its wealth and power. Of countries not belonging to the center of the capitalist system or not directly affiliated with it, only Japan has fully reached this goal. Nevertheless, Japanese policies, both internal and foreign, up to its military humiliation by the Americans in 1945, show clearly enough that before that date the empire of the rising sun did not consider itself in the least to be a member of the Western "club." Its success has put Japan in a class apart, distinct from the Third World, but no insightful student of history would believe that Japan's national goals and profound yearnings have been satisfied by mere economic success: It is probable that deep inside themselves the Japanese have not abandoned the expectation that in the future, perhaps in alliance with China, they will in turn become the center of a yet unknown world system. That hope, unfounded or not, makes bearable the price the Japanese are meanwhile paying in having been forced to admit, with feigned humility, that 1941 was too early for their bid for regional and eventual world hegemony.

The Japanese "model" remains unique, as if superhuman. The nations of the Third World are precisely those that until now have not found in themselves the indispensable resources for dynamically (and at the same time constructively) reacting to the challenge of having had imposed upon them by foreigners a world view, values and goals alien from their own traditions. The majority of them do not even have demographic or territorial dimensions that would make them geopolitically important in themselves. Those where one or both of those dimensions exist—India, Indonesia, Bangladesh, Egypt, Nigeria or Brazil—all suffer to a lesser or greater degree from inhibitions and ineptitudes that so far have weighed against the successful adoption of the Western model, that is, a free economy in harmony with democratic and truly representative political institutions. The deadweight of traditions and attitudes rooted in the past is not in itself an insurmountable barrier to development, but to overcome it, it would be necessary to take (against nationalism, in our time a dominant collective passion) a temporary subordinate and complementary position within the world capitalist economy and to act accordingly, as Japan did for a century.

When the Third World Did Not Yet Exist

As an entity, as a problem, as a universal concern and as a determining factor of ideas, emotions, and actions, the Third World has a very recent existence. The attitude toward poverty and the relative impotence of one's own society or of other societies had always been to admit that this was simply a fact of life. For a long time after the prodigious leap of the West, its capitalist, political, cultural, scientific and industrial revolutions (in reality a single organic process) and the resulting Western world hegemony, it was taken for granted that that hegemony and its consequences derived in a natural way from Western superiority. The inescapable corollary was that the situation of non-

Western or marginal Western countries could not improve except by the propagation of the West's ways to the rest of the world. It did not seem shocking or anomalous that there should be a difference between the standard of living of say, France and Egypt, at the time those two countries brushed through the expedition of Bonaparte in 1798. It had not occurred to anyone that such difference was an injustice to be corrected, and not at all that the West was somehow guilty of a situation—the poverty of the Egyptian masses—that had always existed. On the contrary, everybody who gave thought to the matter must have assumed that only if the human energies that had made the West were unleashed in the non-Western world would it begin to pull out of its unquestionable inferiority.[7]

Marx himself, in an 1853 text[8] embarrassing for Third World ideologists who call themselves Marxists, categorically rejects the idea that India, learned, refined and by no means the most backward among the non-Western regions of the world, had suffered a net loss from Western imperialism. The conquest and domination of India by the British had disarticulated the framework of Hindu society. But reactionary sorrow about the disintegration of an ancient way of life must be outweighed, in the view of any modern person, by the recognition that only Western civilization was capable of effecting favorable changes in India, which could only benefit by having been influenced by the Western world. And that was valid for India, must be equally or even more so for the rest of the non-Western world. As for the marginal Western republics that had succeeded the Spanish empire in America, submerged as they were in a state of anarchy that only tyrants could fitfully cope with, it appeared, analogously, that their only hope of improvement lay in whole-hearted acceptance of their Western inheritance and the operation, here also, of European and United States imperialism.

That view of the matter was doubtless ethnocentric and inadequate, but much closer to the truth than the revision of Marx that I have called the Third World ideology, according to which the non-Western and marginal Western peoples have seen their beatitude destroyed by the West. Yet we are by now confronted with overwhelming evidence that such Third Worldism has become the most potent socialist weapon of our time, as Hobson wished and foresaw as early as 1903.

The Emergence of the Third World Question

It is necessary to inquire into the causes of the almost sudden reversal in the perception of the causes and meanings of the differences between nations, from the time when the greatest revolutionary thinker thought that on balance Western imperialism was progressive and the only force that would unchain the human potential of Asia, Africa, and Latin America, to the present, when it is taken as axiomatic that the West is to blame for the backwardness and poverty of the current Third World.

One reason for this reversal is that in recent years the wealth of the West has so immensely increased that the non-Western or marginal Western countries, though much better off from all points of view than in 1853, lag farther behind today in relative terms. Another reason is that the advance in education and in communications has meant that countries that have lagged behind are now aware of their situations in a way that they had not been, and therefore envy and desire the advantages deriving from industrial and technological development. They have also perceived that natural resources either found in their territories or considered the common inheritance of mankind (the oxygen of the atmosphere, oceans, minerals in ocean floors) are used disproportionately and often destructively by the industrialized countries.

The destruction of ancient social orders by the impact of the capitalist system has indeed been, just as Marx predicted, the necessary condition for the launching of modernization, and has given rise to previously unimaginable expectations; but since these have been met only partially, the subjective feeling (which is what counts) is one of having lost something invaluable and irreplaceable without true or sufficient compensation. Objective and measurable improvements owed to policies, to social changes and to technical progress of Western origin or inspiration, appear of little value or are taken for granted and tend to be overshadowed by new tensions caused by those same changes.

The propagation of Christianity as a practiced religious faith or as a diffuse cultural and ideological influence, accompanied by mass education according to the Western model, has drilled into non-Western countries (and especially into their elites) a world view all the more seductive since it is presumed to be organically linked to Western success and power; and also because, as it became evident from the very early success and lightning propagation of the Christian gospel, egalitarianism, historicism, and salvationism are in strong harmony with at least one facet of the complex of human hopes.

And then, there is nationalism. Among the components of the modern Western world view, paramountcy was early gained by nationalism, an idea wrapped in violent emotions that had previously been insignificant or unknown, and which, when transferred to non-Western countries, has acted virulently and made the central contribution to the rise of the Third World question.

Nationalism is an ideology and passion that crystallized in Europe in the eighteenth century. Its catalyst was the French Revolution and the military successes of France starting from the battle of Valmy. The perfectly justified conviction began to emerge that the new strength and pride of the French were due to the rise of a national consciousness among the masses of the population. In contrast, the peoples of Germany, Austria, and Italy remained either parceled into microstates of feudal origin or, conversely, held artificially within one multi–nation-state with no obvious common bond except submission to a single crown. From the reflection on these contrasting realities arose the thesis that mankind is divided by nature into nations, that those nations are recognized by means of certain specific characteristics, and that the only legitimate governments are those that are national and autonomous at the same time.[9]

The characteristics that distinguish nations are cultural and especially linguistic, since language is not a neutral means of communication among men, but rather the crystallization of nationality.[10] Another postulate of the Western-born ideology that is nationalism, is the idea that history is the stage for the fulfillment or frustration of human aspirations. "The nationalist doctrine, upon declaring that the only legitimate political associations are those that speak the same language, share the same culture and venerate the same heroes and the same forefathers, expresses in ideological terms a concern for history that has been converted into the dominant theme of the modern European world view, adopted wherever European culture has penetrated."[11]

Its potency once discovered, the conscious use of nationalism in struggles for power immediately began, first in Europe and then the rest of the world. Napoleon stirred it up in Italy and even tried to use it in Egypt against the Mamelukes. England used it against Napoleon in Spain, and against Spain in the Americas. The expressions "national liberation" and "national unity" for the first time appeared in current verbal usage. This peculiarly Western notion thus began its blazing career, of which we can now perceive that it was destined to succeed, much more than was Marxism, as the dominant ideology in the twentieth century and, ironically, the most potent factor in the erosion and dissolution of Western hegemony.

Ambitious young Asians and Africans from the colonies at first came to London, Paris, Amsterdam or Brussels eager to be Westernized, willing to become bearers of the Western gospel in their home countries. They had taken democratic and liberal ideology seriously. But they were brutally rebuffed by reality, which did not correspond to high Western humanist and Christian ideas but to Western nationalist chauvinism, xenophobia and racism. The lesson was not wasted: sadder, older and much wiser, they returned to their nations and turned into nationalist agitators against Western domination. Later some of them would become the revolutionary leaders, the national heroes and finally the rulers of decolonized nations after 1945.

By the way, it is nowadays held as part of the Third World ideology that racism is a Western and, moreover, modern Western capitalist sin. The truth of the matter is that racism has never been absent from human society.[12] What has happened is that just as with other sources of tension and conflict, racism has become a big issue in the unprecedentedly global context created by the capitalist revolution. Racism, as many other evils of a similar or worse nature known by humanity from time immemorial, used to be equitably endured or even accepted because they were considered to be eternal and immutable. Today those evils are very much noticed and even taken to be novel and unprecedented because incompatible with the ideals of welfare and equality (and the reality of mass prosperity) formulated and partially realized by capitalist civilization. In the case of racism it is, moreover, in flagrant contradiction with the ethic of the gospels. Therefore, there was a shocking contradiction between the teachings of Christian missionaries and the practices of European administrators and tradesmen in the colonies. Against white racism, it was natural that the new nationalism of the colonized peoples would invent a backlash antiwhite racism that has become one of the most virulent components of the Third World ideology.[13]

The Suicide of Europe

The series of nationalist wars and the social, economic and political crises that shook the West and which reached a climax with World War II, cracked beyond repair the mirror in which the colonized saw themselves as imperfect and inferior Europeans. European prestige began to erode fast as early as the Russo-Japanese war (1904-5) which, in addition to being an important link in the chain of events that led to the Bolshevik Revolution, also meant the first victory of a nonwhite nation against a European power. Black populations in West Africa, totally ignorant of international affairs, became excited in 1906 with the rumor that such a surprising breach of normality had occurred the year before in a distant sea.

Less than ten years later, World War I offered the spectacle of an orgy of senseless killing between European states that until that time had presented themselves as models of civilization for all mankind. Some of the belligerents brought colonial contingents to fight on European soil, where they could witness first hand that war of the West against itself. The war had as immediate corollaries the destruction of the Russian, Austrian, and Ottoman Empires, and the Bolshevik Revolution. The latter was actually stimulated by the Germans with the purpose of easing the pressure on their eastern front (just as the British had sent Colonel Lawrence and other agents to promote rebellion in the Arab provinces in the Ottoman Empire). But the Russian Revolution had its own course to follow, and among its most important consequences would be to give theoretical formulation and material aid to nationalist and anti-Western feeling in the colonial and dependent countries.

In the West itself, the period between the two world wars was one of anxiety, questioning, disillusionment, bitterness, inflation, economic depression, unemployment, social conflicts and political aberrations. States previously strong and apparently serene saw their bases shaken and the legitimacy of their governments questioned. The Marxist prediction that capitalism would strangle the very productive forces that it had unleashed seemed about to be fulfilled. The ruling classes, so recently arrogant, could not hide the fact that they had lost their self-assurance and their faith in their political opinions. Therefore, in Italy and Germany they easily yielded to the temptation of abdicating power into the hands of Mussolini and Hitler. That triumph of fascism in two such centrally Western countries as Germany and Italy, and its absurd prestige in France in the 1930s, seemed to signal the irreversible decline of democracy in Europe. Nazi Germany supposedly offered the example of the forseeable evolution of every advanced capitalist country, and proof that redemption from that fate could only come by means of the communist revolution. When in 1939 Europe again went to war against itself, it seemed to have abdicated all right to present itself as a paradigm of civilization. And it did condemn itself to lose what remained of its past worldwide political hegemony.

In this conflict the Europeans again used their colonies. But this time they had to hint or clearly offer that after the war, such cooperation would have its reward in degrees of self-determination up to near or outright independence. Furthermore, Japan proved with its victories in the Pacific and by replacing British, Dutch and French colonial governments that nonwhite people could not only defeat whites but also run public affairs efficiently. At first indigenous populations received the

Japanese rather favorably, in spite of their arrogance and cruelty; an ominous fact that the West preferred not to understand, as it failed to see that movements of national resistance were a complementary, not countervailing, factor to Japanese prestige. Both accelerated the development of a militant nationalism and counterracism, and would be catalysts of an irresistible drive toward independence from the first day after Japanese defeat.

Moreover, it was to be expected that postwar political arrangements would above all take into account the opinions, prejudices, obligations, interests, and strategic considerations of the two great victors of the war, the United States and the Soviet Union. Divided in practically everything else, the new dominant world powers agreed that the European colonial system should be dismantled, and that they would support the exacerbated nationalism of the colonized countries. In the case of the United States, this atttitude was based on its own history as a former colony that had won its freedom in a war of national liberation, and on its traditional mistrust and even hostility toward the European powers. Also, the United States had up to that time an ill-founded image of itself as free of imperialist sins; it did not dream that its so-called protection of Latin America, starting from the formulation of the Monroe Doctrine, was in many ways an analog of European imperialism in Asia and Africa. The Soviet Union had its own powerful and very well thought-out motives for desiring the most abrupt decolonization.

The Role of the United Nations

In the immediate postwar period, the above mentioned factors created a political climate in which the non-Western countries suddenly felt much more dissatisfied with their relative situation in the world. Invented about then, the label "Third World" was an instant success, but not so much because of its original intention to exclude Asia and Africa from the contest between the United States and the Soviet Union; rather, very soon—without the new meaning being explicitly noted—because it was used for its conflict-loaded anti-Western fighting words. Thus "Third World" came to categorize all non-Western or marginally Western countries which, having been colonized or dominated by, and in any case fascinated by the West, had virulently contracted the Western passion for nationalism and would thenceforth find it unacceptable to be less "superior" than other countries.

The United Nations organization explicitly included that claim in its founding charter, where the principle of the equality of all sovereign states was incorporated. But since inequality stubbornly persisted, the United Nations also took upon itself the mission of remedying that situation, considered intolerable in the new era. Sundry agencies, committees and subcommittees were dedicated to finding solutions to the inequality between nations, and produced in a few years a mountain of literature on development and underdevelopment. Many years went by before those millions of words were to receive the verdict that they deserved, paradoxically delivered by someone who had himself been one of the high priests of the cult, Gunnar Myrdal. With admirably self-critical spirit, although somewhat belatedly, Myrdal eventually reached the conclusion that the mass of that literature on development had essentially been "diplomatic, indulgent and generally too optimistic: it omitted the facts on each occasion when they would have provoked uncomfortable problems, camouflaging them under a pseudo-technical terminology or else dealing with them with clemency and with (condescending) comprehension."[14]

It could not have happened otherwise. Any diagnosis of the then recently discovered phenomenon of "under-development" (a term in itself euphemistic) that had frankly recognized the intrinsic causes of the inequalities among nations, would have directly affronted the nationalist tidal wave and its fervent mythology. The so-called development experts in the UN, the universities, the media, would not have kept their jobs for a minute if they had been so reckless as to offend a convulsed non-Western world with the proposition that its problems were largely indigenous; or with the gentlest exhortation to confront them self-critically and realistically. Communist bred and nurtured Third World ideology now came into its own. It was marvelously convenient to hold that backwardness is never the fault of those who suffer it, but always of some foreign demon; not the necessary result of ancient obscurantism, but rather the unjust and fortuitous consequence of yesterday's colonialism.

In that emotional and pseudointellectual climate of passions and false social sciences, of spontaneous fires eagerly fed with the tinder of spurious but seductive theories, the national liberation movements of the Third World acquired an irresistible force and were indiscriminantly acclaimed by well-intentioned opinion, even in those cases when they were being transparently manipulated by the Soviet Union. This situation remains virtually unchanged today, although those national liberation movements have engendered uniformly tyrannical and incompetent governments. We see how so-called progressive opinion continues to adulate or at least refrain from criticizing former guerrillas though they have turned into tyrants or corrupt bureaucrats. For liberals in the United States, Third World rulers are judged not by any improvement they make in the freedom and welfare of their countries (areas where almost invariable and in many cases catastrophic regression has occurred) but by the contribution they have made and are still making to the weakening of an "unjust" international order—in other words, their contribution to the eventual destruction of the world capitalist system.

The Suicide of the West

Our analysis of the causes and consequences of the rise of the Third World and of the Third World ideology, the one as a central problem and the other as a key ideology of our time, would be seriously incomplete if limited to the ideas and emotions of the non-Western and marginal Western countries, leaving aside the fact that both the entity (the Third World) and the corresponding ideology (the Third World ideology) were essentially Western creations, wrought and passionately discussed in the first place in the West and only much later, as a consequence, by the countries that were the object of that discussion. Furthermore, the issue has been and remains a powerful agent of agitation, self-flagellation, and political dissolution in the heart of the Western societies. The term "proletarian nations" that some propagandists have proposed to substitute for the less virulent "Third World" is a clear statement of the role that countries so labeled are expected to play in history. Consciously or not, the Western community itself has come to accept as axiomatic the affirmation that Western countries solely, principally or at least decisively owe their development to their having exploited the proletarian countries; and that the capitalist system is essentially a mechanism of confiscation by the former of the surplus value produced by the work of the latter, and of the natural resources found in Third World territories. An astonishing number of Western opinion makers (writers, journalists, academics) are secretly or openly persuaded that they and their fellow citizens owe their relative well-being to shameful abuses committed by their countries against the Third World. They also seem to feel that as a consequence, Western civilization is disqualified, fundamentally inhuman and corrupt; deserves to be punished and even destroyed; and, finally, that it cannot regain (or acquire for the first time) true humanity unless it surrenders politically and psychologically to the values and supposedly superior world view of the "oppressed countries," exactly in the way that the bourgeoisie was to be saved by the proletariat in the Marxist morality play.[15]

Such feelings of masochistic guilt and death-wish neurosis reached sad and grotesque extremes in the white women who became converts and auxiliaries of violent and event lunatic black power movements, including the middle-class Englishwoman, Gale Benson, alias Hale-Kimga, who was murdered in Trinidad in 1972[16]; or the servants of "socialist" sects, such as the People's Temple, whom the "Reverend" Jim Jones dragged into collective suicide in his commune in Jamestown, Guyana, in 1978. These extreme cases are a symptom of a malaise that has profoundly penetrated the soul of the Western societies and could become their ruin, not only because of the aid and comfort that it gives to Soviet expansionism and influence in the Third World, but primarily for its internal effect in fostering Western discouragement, apathy, and paralyzing guilt. This defeatism began in the ranks of the liberal or outright Marxist intelligentsia and in the universities and has propagated to all vital and influential sectors of Western society: the non-Marxist political parties, the Church, labor unions, the government bureaucracy, the press, the affluent, the middle class, the young and sooner or later, the armed forces.

The West appearing to have lost its nerve, one must wonder whether the Third World challenge will be met, as prudence and justice recommend, by the bold reform of an international economic order that would remain essentially capitalist. This is a reform in which the advanced capitalist countries would cede to qualified Third World countries some of their advantages, fairly or unfairly acquired, with a corresponding defusing of the so-called international social question. In the absence or failure of such an accommodation, however, the Soviet Union can continue to exploit the resentment of the Third World against the West until the capitalist world system becomes cornered and readied for the kill.[17] This destruction of capitalist civilization, if it occurs, will have been caused, as always in history, more by internal factors than by foreign challenges, and to a large extent by the growth within the body of Western societies, as a cancer, of the Third World ideology.

Notes

Parts of this chapter appeared in the magazines *Politique Internationale* 3 (Spring 1979):67-83; *Commentaire* 9 (Spring 1980):105-10; and *The Jerusalem Journal of International Relations,* vol. 4, no. 2 (1979): 16-30.

1. The following quotation from Stalin is also relevant (and piquant, since it refers to Afghanistan):

   > The road of victory of the [Communist] revolution in the West lies through revolutionary alliance with the liberation movement of the colonies and dependent countries against imperialism. . . . The revolutionary character of a national movement . . . does not presuppose the existence of proletarian elements in the movement, the existence of a revolutionary of a republican program of the movement, the existence of a democratic basis of the movement. The struggle the Emir of Afghanistan is waging for the independence of Afghanistan is objectively a revolutionary struggle, despite the monarchist views of the Emir and his associates, for it weakens, disintegrates, and undermines imperialism. . . . For the same reasons, the struggle the Egyptian merchants and bourgeois intellectuals are waging for the independence of Egypt is objectively a revolutionary struggle, despite . . . the fact that they are opposed to socialism; whereas . . . the British Labor Government . . . is . . . *reactionary,* despite the proletarian origin and the proletarian title of the members of that government (since it administers the national interests of an advanced capitalist country). . . . Lenin was right in saying that the national movement of the oppressed countries should be appraised not from the point of view of formal democracy but from the point of view of the actual results obtained, as shown by the general balance sheet of the struggle against imperialism. (See Joseph Stalin, "Foundations of Leninism," in *Problems of Leninism* [Moscow: 1945], pp. 59-67.)

2. For the complete text of the "Theses of the Second Congress of the Communist International on the National and Colonial Questions," see Elie Kedourie, *Nationalism in Asia and Africa* (London: Weidenfeld & Nicholson, 1971), pp. 540-51.

3. "The Third World . . . consists of dominated and exploited countries, called 'underdeveloped,' dependent on the capitalist system. They include: (a) the countries of Latin America, that is, all of America including the Caribbean and with the sole exception of the United States and Canada, capitalist and developed, and of socialist Cuba; (b) all Africa; (c) all Asia and Oceania, except, on the one hand, some socialist countries (China, North Korea, North Vietnam, Soviet Asia and Mongolia) and, on the other hand, some developed capitalist countries (Japan, Israel, Australia, and New Zealand)." (See: Pierre Jalée, *le Tiers Monde en chiffres,* Maspéro: Paris, 1971). Today Jalée would exclude from the Third World, South Vietnam, Cambodia, Laos, Afghanistan, Angola, Ethiopia, and Nicaragua, for the sole reason that they have passed under the domination of some variety of Marxist-Leninist socialism. And he would include Taiwan, Singapore, and South Korea in the "imperialist camp," because these three Asiatic countries have in the meantime shaken themselves loose from the Third World neurosis.

4. For a full development of this concept, see Carlos Rangel, *The Latin Americans: Their Love-Hate Relationship with the United States* (New York: Harcourt Brace Jovanovich, 1977), pp. 100-140.

5. Jean-François Revel, "L'Amérique Latine et sa culture politique," *Commentaire* 3 (Fall 1978):261-66.

6. For example, the speech of President Carter before the Organization of American States on April 14, 1977.
7. This actually happened in Japan. This country reacted to the incursion of United States Commander Matthew Perry in 1853 with the deliberate project of modernizing, which in practice could mean only "Westernizing," thus demonstrating, if such a demonstration were necessary, that its underdevelopment and its weakness up to that time were not due to an intromission of Western imperialism, but rather that intromission shook Japanese society from a lethargic condition, and inaugurated for Japan a new era of dynamism and creativity.
8. Karl Marx, *The British Rule in India,* and *The Future Results of Brtish Rule in India* (1853). Marx stressed that rural life in India was far less idyllic than was generally believed, for

> we must not forget that these idyllic village communties, inoffensive though they may appear, had always been the solid foundation of Oriental despotism, that they restrained the human mind within the smallest possible compass, making it the unresisting tool of superstition, enslaving it beneath traditional rules, depriving it of all grandeur and historical energies. We must not forget the barbarian egotism which, concentrating on some miserable patch of land, had quietly witnessed the ruin of empires, the perpetration of unspeakable cruelties, the massacre of the population of large towns, with no other consideration bestowed upon them than on natural events, itself the helpless prey of any aggressor who deigned to notice it at all. We must not forget that this undignified, stagnatory, and vegetative life, that this passive sort of existence evoked on the other part, in contradistinction, wild, aimless, unbounded forces of destruction and rendered murder itself a religious rite in Hindustan. We must not forget that these little communities were contaminated by distinctions of caste, and by slavery, that they subjugated man to external circumstances instead of elevating man into the sovereign of circumstances, that they tranformed a self-developing social state into never-changing natural destiny, and thus brought about a brutalizing worship of nature. . . . Arabs, Turks, Tartars, Moguls, who had successively overrun India, soon became Hindooized, the barbarian conquerors being, by the eternal law of history, conquered themselves by the superior civilization of their subjects. The British were the first conquerors superior, and therefore, inaccessible to Hindoo civilization.

> Marx went on to enumerate the several ways in which a superior culture, Western culture, could not help but provoke a whole series of desirable transformations in India, thus launching progress of every kind in a region of the earth that was obviously backward and quite inferior to what it would doubtlessly become once it had been in Marx's words, "annexed to the Western world." Marx stated that the following benefits had accrued to India, or were soon to accrue to India, thanks to the impact of the West: political unity; the recruitment and training of a native army; printing and freedom of expression, "introduced for the first time into Asiatic society;" the possibility of simple citizens' acquiring land (Marx viewed the princes' monopoly over land

ownership as the worst blight in Asian society); Western-style education, whose consequences, already perceptible in 1853, were leading to
the development of "a fresh class . . . endowed with the requirements
for government and imbued with European science"; the telegraph;
steam, "which has brought India into regular and rapid communication
with Europe, has connected its chief ports with those of the whole
south-eastern ocean, and has revindicated it from the isolated position
which was the prime law of its stagnation"; irrigation; and finally a
railroad network, which was to provide the springboard for modern
industrial development, since "you cannot maintain a net of railways
over an immense country without introducing all those industrial
processes necessary to meet the immediate and current wants of
railway locomotion, and out of which there must grow the application
of machinery to those branches of industry not immediately connected
with railways." (Quoted in Miklós Molnar, *Marx, Engels et la politique
internationale* [Paris: Gallimard, 1975]).

9. Elie Kedourie, *Nationalism in Asia and Africa,* (London: Weidenfeld &
Nicholson, 1971), p. 28.
10. Ibid., p. 34.
11. Ibid., p. 35.
12. To verify the existence of a severe anti-Black racism in the best moments
of Islamic civilization, it is sufficient to leaf through *The Arabian Nights.*
13. The following text is illustrative on this racism in reverse, and its affinity
with the Third World ideology:

Often we are asked why we haven't united our efforts with the white
workers of the U.S. We don't do it not only because of the racism of
U.S. whites and of the white working class in particular, but also
because the white working class is an integral part of U.S. society. . . .
When the white working class of the U.S. organized, its struggle was
not for the control of the means of production or for the redistribution
of wealth. Its struggle was simply to obtain more money. The capitalists of the U.S. decided, with the purpose of obtaining even more
profits and at the same time avoiding the inevitable class conflict that
Marx refers to, to exploit the Third World. Their profits increased, and
they threw the crumbs to the white working class, which accepted
them. Therefore, the white working class also came to enjoy the profit
obtained with the sweat of the Third World, by which they became an
integral part of the system and they have to fight beside the capitalists
to maintain it.

We black Americans are allies of the people of the Third World because
we consider ourselves to be, and in reality we are, a colony within the
very United States, in the same way that the people of the Third World
are colonies outside the U.S. The same power structure that exploits
and oppresses the Third World exploits and oppresses us. Therefore,
our enemy is the same and in reality the only way that we can be
liberated will be when we unite and defeat our common enemy. We are
not fighting against Capitalism (in one country); we are fighting against
international Capitalism; and just as the imperialist powers of the world

have internationalized their system, we must also internationalize ours, so that our struggle becomes an international struggle.

That's why the words of Che (Guevara), when he says that we must create two, three or more Viet Nams, have such an important meaning.

We visualize (Imperialism) as an enormous octopus, whose tentacles extend throughout the world, and whose eye is in the U.S. Cuba has already cut one of its tentacles; Viet Nam has tied another; nevertheless, the rest of the tentacles are loose, and each time that a struggle begins, the octopus immediately stretches out other tentacles. . . . If we black Americans could get other countries to tie down other tentacles, we would take advantage, and while those tentacles were occupied, we could stab the eye of the octopus. That would be our work. . . . If we allow the U.S. to continue waging a fight here, and then another there, it would (resist) indefinitely; but if we force the U.S. to fight in several fronts at the same time, it will be possible to defeat it almost immediately. In this lies, precisely, the importance of the Third World.

If the people of the different non-white races who have been exploited by the white man, whether Chinese, Indian or black were to unite, understanding that we are the majority of mankind and that the white man is in the minority . . . we would no longer be afraid of the white man.

If the poeple of Malaysia, of Somalia, Portuguese Guinea, of Venezuela, of Brazil, of Viet Nam—everyone, including the black people of the U.S.—decided to unite and to fight, we could defeat the Western powers in a short time. . . . We have hatred for the West—the type of hatred to which Che refers—which will turn us into efficient and cold killing machines. . . . We will make the U.S. to go up in flames, and then we will sit like Nero and see it burn. (Stokely Carmichael, "El Tercer Mundo, nuestro mundo," *Tricontinental* [July-August 1967]:15-22.)

14. Gunnar Myrdal, *The Challenge of World Poverty* (London: Pelican, 1971), pp. 26, 28.
15. See, for example, the prologue of Jean-Paul Sartre to *The Wretched of the Earth*, by Franz Fanon.
16. See, V. S. Naipaul, "Michael X and the murders in Trinidad," in *The Return of Eva Péron* (New York: Knopf, 1980), pp. 3-91.
17. The national question may in the end turn against Russia, white and semi-European, and could eventually result in the dissolution of the Soviet empire and even of the Soviet Union itself. But that would be another story.

4

Capitalism and the Third World

The charges against capitalism and its influence upon the Third
World are, in synthesis, that poor countries today are worse off than
ever before, or even that they were once in a state of near perfect social
harmony and economic equilibrium, having lost this bliss entirely
because of the complementarity that the imperialist countries have
forced on them. In other words, the developed world is rich because
the underdeveloped world is poor, and vice versa. We would witness a
general situation in which the progress of some countries compared to
other countries, but also the backwardness of the latter in opposition to
the former, would be essentially explained by the reciprocal effect of
the economic, cultural, and political exchanges between the advanced
on the one hand and the backward on the other.[1] Thus the links
between all regions of the globe, established for the first time by
capitalism, are held by the Third World ideology to have been exclusively advantageous for the capitalist centers, and exclusively detri-
mental to the peripheries; if those links had never been established,
England perhaps would be as backward as India, or India as advanced
as England, or both would have a comparable degree of prosperity,
inferior to present day England, but superior to present day India.

To achieve the process by which they become and remain rich at the
expense of others, the imperial countries would have deliberately
degraded Third World countries and falsely persuaded them of their
intrinsic inferiority. Through this clever Western trick, the consequences of imperialist exploitation, evident in the inequality of nations,
could be attributed to that supposed inferiority and not to the true
cause which is imperial exploitation, first through colonialism and
more recently through neocolonialism and dependency.

All these allegations, fundamental to the Third World ideology, are
false in general and false in each aspect. The Third World's poorest
countries are not those that have had longer and closer exchanges with

the West, but, significantly, those whose exchanges have been weaker and shorter—Ethiopia, for instance. Until 1935, when it was invaded by fascist Italy, Ethiopia had never suffered Western contacts other than the passing through of some European eccentrics searching for the sources of the Nile. There was, it is true, a British expedition (1867-68) to rescue some of those explorers held prisoner by Emperor Theodore, a military display which, its mission accomplished, turned its heels and went home. And there was a first Italian attempt at invasion (in 1896) so ragged that it was easily rejected by the Ethiopians.

The appalling poverty and backwardness of Ethiopia continue unabated or worse. These conditions—although it is no longer fashionable to recall them, since that country has now fallen into the Soviet orbit—therefore owe nothing to Western influence. In sharp contrast is Nigeria, where, prior to 1890, there was no cultivation of cocoa, peanuts or cotton. Due to the British development and commercialization of their cultivation, however, Nigeria today exports an enormous proportion of the world supply of these products. Another example, among many, is what occurred in Malaya (today part of Malaysia), which, at the end of the nineteenth century, remained a wretchedly sparsely populated territory, where practically the only economic activity was fishing by primitive methods. By the time it achieved independence in 1963 (in federation with Singapore, Sarawak, and Borneo), Malaya had become a prosperous and populous nation due to the British colonial administrations' introduction of the cultivation of rubber.

The Terms of Trade

The Third World ideology reflects in terms of current world politics a very old fallacy present in all of the reincarnations of the socialist animus: the conviction that enrichment by fair means and personal or national virtues is just not possible, so that the wealth of an individual or community cannot be in any way the just result of their special and honest efforts and ingenuity, but must have been confiscated from others, who consequently must suffer a degree of impoverishment equivalent to the prosperity of their exploiters. With reference to this fallacy, the tyrants of several of the new African states unleashed a vast repression of ethnic minorities, mainly Indians, who had achieved—thanks to their diligence and capacity as tradesmen and artisans—relative prosperity compared to that of the Black populations. The ruin and expulsion of these minorities, carried out for example by Idi Amin Dada in Uganda under the allegation that they had prospered by exploiting and robbing the Black population, caused suffering and impoverishment not only among these "colored Jews," but also among the native Ugandans. In fact, Uganda remains even today an example of wretched poverty and mass suffering, clearly caused not by the colonial relationship but by its termination.

One Third World allegation taken as irrefutable is the affirmation that the terms of trade between the Third World and the industrialized countries are continually deteriorating. This is true in some cases, not quite so in others, and plainly false when taken to explain the difficulties in the balance of payments within the group of countries labeled Third World. In many factual instances the international price of raw materials has had a medium- and long-range tendency to increase in relation to the price of manufactured products, so that over time the value of beef or wheat, the traditional exports to Argentina, has increased more than the value of, say, tractors or computers. To get Argentina into trouble it took a purposefully perverse economic policy followed by consecutive Argentinan governments contemptuous of agriculture and committed to pursuing an illusory industrial autarchy. It was not the deterioration in the terms of trade that set Argentina back, from a situation comparable or better than that of countries with similar economies such as Canada, Australia, and New Zealand, to the virtually irreparable mess left behind by the second Peronist government. Significantly, it was Peron who declared upon his return in 1973, after twenty years exile, that Argentina was now a Third World country, a sad substitution for a modernization project that one hundred years earlier had aimed to pull Argentina up on the same level with Europe. Even sadder is to recall that the now discarded ambition to put Argentina in the first ranks of world nations had been conceived and partially and promisingly carried out.

Of course, the story of oil prices is the most notable factual refutation of the proposition that the fluctuation in the terms of trade invariably work in favor of the industrialized countries and against the exporters of raw materials. For decades, oil had yielded growing revenues for the exporting countries, but since 1973 prices have increased tenfold. Such is the stubbornness of Third World ideologists: they unblinkingly persist in denouncing the deterioration of the terms of trade as one of the main forms of extortion used by imperialism against the Third World, ignoring the fact that the explosion in oil prices is the greatest setback ever experienced in international trade by poor countries that are not oil producers—of course, the overwhelming majority.

The Foreign Debt

Another war horse of the Third World ideology is the foreign debt of Asia, Africa and Latin America, regarded somehow as perversely inflicted on those countries by the United States, Great Britain, France, Germany, Switzerland, etc., when obviously the origin of that debt was the transference of real resources from lending to borrowing countries, under conditions frequently more advantageous both in installments and interest rates than those prevailing in the international financial markets. The thesis is just short of ridiculous that private Western and Japanese banks (but also the World Bank and the International Monetary Fund) meant to harm the Third World with their loans. But it is less surprising that that argument be put forward and be taken seriously if we realized that for radical Third World ideologists, even outright grants by the West to the Third World are harmful, since they maintain dependency and postpone the magical day of the final and irreversible split with imperialism.

Viewing the foreign debt of the Third World objectively, it is evident that the incapacity of certain countries to productively use the immense real resources that have been transferred to them from the advanced capitalist countries since 1945, is another symptom among many that reveals the typical ineptitude and large scale corruption of the majority of the Third World governments. The bankers' inexcusable sin was to lend such astronomical sums to such unworthy borrowers. Just as in the previously mentioned fallacy according to which there can be no just enrichment, and neither individual nor collective prosperity would be feasible except by despoiling others, there also exists with equal tenacity the natural resentment of debtors against lenders. Typically, a fool who has mortgaged his house to invest in an unprofitable business or to gamble, without thinking of the due date of the loan, will say upon losing his house that the bank robbed him. In the case of nation-states, the private banks or the international credit agencies do not have the possibility of "foreclosing the mortgages," and paradoxically have to worry a great deal more than the debtor governments over conditions of virtual bankruptcy caused by the same perversity as that of the fool who mortgaged his house.

The more tolerant the lender, the greater will be the rancor of the debtor. The private banks which in a display of folly lent money excessively to Third World countries must be ruthless bargainers, lest their executive officers suffer the just ire of stockholders. Yet they have not been held up to excessive obloquy, because they could react by closing credit to governments that defame them. But the International

Monetary Fund is an international agency and an institution that can be qualified as philanthropic. Therefore it is incapable, by definition, of taking offense at the torrent of abuse hurled against it. It can thus be used as a scapegoat and crucified for the sins of both lenders and borrowers. If it did not exist, it would have to be invented.

The Case of Jamaica

Under the despised British colonial administration, Jamaica was a prosperous society. In 1970, its per capita GNP was about $700—equal to that of Mexico and more than twice that of Brazil. It had a reasonably diversified agriculture and a virtual absence of illiteracy. Life expectancy was among the highest in the world (seventy years) since a reasonably well-fed population enjoyed an excellent health service. In addition, Jamaica was a political democracy and was accustomed to civilized coexistence. Such was the inheritance left by the British colonial administration. Since 1970 Jamaica derived additional benefits from substantial exports of bauxite and alumina, the increasing prices of which partly compensated for the higher prices of the oil that Jamaica must import. Sugar, another important export product, doubled its price in 1974 and again in 1975.

It should have been impossible to ruin Jamaica, but that was precisely the singular achievement of the socialist, Third World ideologist government of the charismatic and handsome Michael Manley, a paradigm in many ways of the type of leader that the majority of new independent nations has produced since 1945. Manley rose to power in 1972. Under his leadership (if it can be called that) Jamaica's GNP decreased year after year for a total of 16 percent during the seven years between 1973-79. Furthermore, due to population growth, GNP in those years fell, relative to the greater number of Jamaicans, by about 25 percent. By 1979 unemployment had risen to over 30 percent. What had been a peaceful and attractive island became a bitter and violent place. Xenophobic antagonism in the streets frightened away most of the foreign tourism that had been a mainstay of the economy.

In 1973 Jamaica's foreign debt was only about $300 million, its service representing only 6 percent of export revenues. Seven years later, the number rose to 90 percent of export revenues due to a combination of a decrease in exports and a galloping increase in the foreign debt.

Is Michael Manley to blame for this wreckage of what was one of the most solid and promising economies of the Third World? The rational answer is clearly yes, because of his disastrous "socialistic" economic policies. Further, his fatuous public flattery of Fidel Castro and the "Cuban model"[2] finished off all probability of private investment in Jamaica.

Nevertheless, Third World ideology blames Jamaica's trouble under Manley on the International Monetary Fund for having lent Jamaica money and having dared to demand rationality in its economic policy before lending it more. In March 1980, Manley ostentatiously wrote to the IMF, blaming it for Jamaica's difficulties and accusing it of being an agency expressly dedicated to undermining Third World economy. Immediately after he called for elections, with which he showed that his quarrel with the IMF, that "imperialist tool," was instrumental to his reelection campaign, and incidentally an additional step toward the ruin of Jamaica.[3]

The Demonstration Effect

The so-called demonstration effect is another expedient, this time indirect, for blaming the Third World's backwardness on the developed world. According to this theory, if Africa, Asia, and Latin America did not have constantly before their eyes the performance of the advanced capitalist countries, they would be happy, and would enjoy a balanced, prosperous and free development. The capitalist countries, because of their very existence as such, and because images of the capitalist lifestyle have been widely broadcast via mass media, have distorted the expectations of this Third World and the economic behavior of its private and public sectors. The radical ending (*brutal* is a more appropriate word) of this bad influence, by closing frontiers and by censorship, would be one of the benefits of the panacea of socialist revolution and its break with imperialism. Fidel Castro's actions in Cuba provide an example of this.

Yet the result has not been, in fact, the extinction from the soul of the Cuban people of the yearning for better living conditions, but (as in other countries submitted to that endless quarantine) a mythification of life in the capitalist countries. Since these prisoners no longer know capitalist civilization first hand, they not only think it vastly superior to socialism, which is of course true, but even go all the way to thinking that it is a perfect system. A former so-called demonstration effect derived from somewhat accurate information is substituted with totally noxious greater dissatisfaction, since it is based on fantasies similar to those suffered by lifers.

All those (politicians, economists, sociologists) who dream of abolishing the demonstration effect in fact desire the coercive use of the state's power to force people's behavior in a given direction, postulated by them to be preferable to what people spontaneously choose. Blocking out all information about the way other countries live will supposedly make the job easier. Maybe this is so and does reinforce the stony stability of governments incapable of giving real satisfaction to the people they rule. But it is highly questionable, in this case as in all others, that the confiscation of freedom can ever be truly beneficial to the welfare of society.

Cuba, for instance, (according to exiled Cuban writer Carlos Alberto Montaner) has been as if "frozen on the magical year 1959."[4] The island lives oppressed by the revolutionary mythology, with its back turned to everything that has happened in the rest of the world since then. Montaner adds: "I was going to write 'in the non-communist world' but it would not be enough. Cubans have had no information about the workers' strikes that took place in Poland in the summer of 1980. The student movement of the 1960s, including May 1968 in Paris, was censored in Cuba. The new ideas, the latest poetry, the latest cinema, experimental theater, avent-garde literature, anti-psychiatry, militant feminism, sexual liberation, the rebirth of religiosity, spiritual orientalism, the rediscovery of Nietzsche, Zen, the recognition of subcultures and counter-cultures, experiments with hallucinogens: everything trivial or important, stupid or profound, noxious or beneficial that has happened in our time has been kept from Cubans."[5]

The Brain Drain

The so-called brain drain is another accusation against the advanced capitalist countries, in the inventory of Western sins which the Third World ideology brandishes as its blanket explanation for everything that ails the Third World. Here again, the socialist revolution has the instant medicine, which is to simply prohibit the emigration of men and women who are in good health and educated, and at the same time encourage the exile of those who because of their age or illness have given all they could to the construction of socialism and have nothing more to be squeezed out. The Soviet Union persists in providing the example. Communist Germany sells refugees to Federal Germany. Cuba achieved a sort of perfection in the application of this so-called socialist humanism when it took advantage of the stampede of refugees to the Peruvian Embassy in Havana to organize the Mariel Operation and get rid of more than one hundred thousand human beings who were considered by the regime to be in some way or other undesirable. Or perhaps we should give Vietnam first prize because of its treatment of the Boat People, deprived of all their valuables in exchange for little vessels in which they sailed toward death on the high seas or, with luck, to be herded by Thailand or Indonesia into horrible refugee camps.

It is true and tragic that the new nation-states of Africa and Asia, and recently some not so new Latin American nation-states, have lost a large number of capable adults who have chosen to live in the advanced capitalist countries. But the blame for this voluntary exile belongs only passively to the countries receiving this transfusion of human resources. These countries have become attractive enough that foreigners, including nonwhites, with some skills are inclined, totally unnaturally, to giving up everything to try to emigrate to such countries rather than remain in their native societies. Major involuntary blame belongs to those unfortunate native societies, whose customs and traditions, in every case older than the earliest contact with the West, discourage and (after decolonization) even punish precisely the characteristic qualities of the protagonists of the brain drain. And an active and perversely voluntary blame can be placed on some Third World governments for deliberately adopting nontraditional, furiously modern, supposedly socialist policies that are incentives to emigration if not actual threats of persecution, literally forcing the attempted emigration of the educated and capable population segment.[6]

The extermination of that "class" in Cambodia is the paradigm of that suicidal side effect of the Third World ideology, the monstrous extreme of a plight experienced by the Chinese minority of Vietnam, by the Indian minority of Uganda, or by the middle and professional classes of Cuba.[7]

Transnational Man

The perverse ambivalence prevailing in the Third World toward the same individuals whose emigration is lamented, blaming the advanced capitalist countries for it and calling it the brain drain, is shown by the difficulties that graduates usually find upon returning from Europe or the United States to their native countries. Those difficulties are sometimes diffuse and noninstitutionalized: for instance, a doctor in philosophy from Heidelberg, or a demographer from the Sorbonne will not be hired by state universities. But in many cases the obstacles are legal and almost insurmountable. In Venezuela, not the most xenophobic or irrational of the countries that call themselves or allow themselves to be counted Third World, it is extremely difficult to revalidate a degree obtained abroad, and this is true even of native-born Venezuelans. In 1974, the Venezuelan government decided to invest a great deal of money in scholarships to thousands of young people and to send them to Europe and the United States to study skills which were scarce in the country. But, contradictorily, the Venezuelan Congress has balked at legislation exempting these young people from the highly troublesome and irrational procedures involving the revalidation of degrees.

The topic of the brain drain has found an unexpected seasoning in recent theories of Latin American sociologists who have coined the phrase "transnational man" to label and discredit Latin American, African, and Asian graduates from European and North American universities.

Actually this is a corollary of the theory of dependence (to which the Latin American social scientists have made such a disproportionate contribution). In synthesis, the scholarships offered by the advanced capitalist countries to young people from the Third World and, of course (and much more sadly), a program involving the funding of the scholarships by the students' home countries, such as the one that Venezuela initiated in 1974, would be "mechanisms for the socio-cultural incorporation to transnational capitalism."[8] The finished product, according to this point of view, will be individuals useful not to their own countries, but to capitalism and to imperialism.

It is not without interest that a paradigm of transnational men should be recognized in Japanese corporate executives. One easily imagines the disdain that Latin American university professors of a socialist bent feel for those termites with slanted eyes, with their poorly cut suits, their synthetic fiber shirts, and their imitation leather briefcases. How elegant, in contrast, to wear English tweed jackets, and to smoke a pipe on some North American campus. But for Japan and the rest of the world the engineers, managers and salesmen of Sony or Honda have been considerably less harmful (to say the least) than their fathers and grandfathers, conquerors of Manchuria and perpetrators of the massacres in Nanking. And I dare to suggest that Chile would have had a less unfortunate recent history had it produced fewer socialist economists and sociologists and more transnational men—on condition, of course, that the latter not be despised and penalized, which is the sure way to wash them down the brain drain.

Bonaparte in Egypt

It is of course true that the present condition of the Third World developed in a complementary way to the rise of the world capitalist system, but not in the sense, usually implicit in that observation, that that process of complementarity has been exclusively prejudicial to the countries of Africa, Asia and Latin America. In previous pages we reflected on the rise of the idea of a Third World and of an international social question. We saw that it has been only very recently that the idea arose that the inequalities in wealth and poverty between nations are an intolerable scandal. All factors that gave rise to this new attitude are of Western origin: the contact between cultures by geographic exploration; the conquest and colonization by Europeans of non-Western territories; the advance in communications that has forged the world (not excluding the Socialist countries) into a single community, where everyone has information about how others live; the demonstration by capitalist social and economic development, more pronounced in some areas of the world community, that poverty, disease, ignorance and extreme social inequalities are not the ineluctable destiny of humanity; and the social tensions generated by modernization.

A certain degree of Third World misery has been caused by the West in this way, without a doubt. Not material poverty, which was much greater before, but rather the painful consciousness of a vast and widening gap between rich and poor, a condition for which the Third World ideology and its fallacies offer compensation. The essential impact of the West on the other countries of the world has been the revelation to those countries of their backwardness. The inevitable result has been painful: a sense of inferiority, of failure, of functioning and living below the suddenly revealed extraordinary potentials of human society, according to the demonstration made by capitalist civilization.

Today we have lost sight of the totally unpredictable and sensational character of that revelation. In this sense the meeting between the Mamalukes and Bonaparte is exemplary. The French had invaded Egypt before, in the twelfth and thirteenth centuries, when the West was actually in a condition of general inferiority to aspects of Moslem civilization, including the art of war. The medieval French knight was a less expert version of the Mamaluke, therefore suffering a severe defeat in battle and having to abandon the ambition to conquer Egypt. During the course of five-and-a-half centuries the Mamalukes remained just as they had always been, and naturally supposed that the French had changed as little. When they learned that Napoleon had had the temerity to land in Alexandria, they made ready to rout him as they had done with Saint Louis in 1250.

But while Egypt had remained virtually static or had degenerated since 1250, the development of capitalist civilization had taken place in

Europe. The result, militarily, was the Battle of the Pyramids. On one side, it was the last cavalry charge of the Middle Ages; on the other side, the rational and methodical use of modern artillery. It was not a battle—it was a massacre.

Both situations, the backwardness of Egypt and the progress of France, had run their course separately. If someone had told the defeated Mamalukes that their military inferiority opposite Napoleon had been caused by Western imperialism, they wouldn't have known what he was talking about.

The Late Competitors

Napoleon's expedition to Egypt has a laboratory-like purity showing with perfect clarity the truth in the controversy about the impact of the West on the Third World. Egypt is today far from being a successful and balanced society; nevertheless, one has to be totally ignorant or completely in bad faith to argue that its situation in 1798 was preferable to what developed thereafter, starting precisely from the French expedition. The result of this was to shake Egypt from its stagnation, but moreover, as is well known, to make it revalue itself. Egypt's extraordinary specificity was a closed book until the explorations and systematic studies were brilliantly made by the scientists and artists whom Bonaparte took along with him. And this is typical of the way capitalist civilization, the only one in history that to a considerable degree has overcome ethnocentrism, has everywhere called to the attention of he non-Western countries their own cultures and identities. Humboldt's travels in the New World and Darwin's in the *Beagle* are as inseparable from the imperialist expansion of the West as the decyphering of the hieroglyphics by Champollion.

France and later England essentially revealed to Egypt alternative possibilities that the Egyptians themselves could not help judging preferable to the tyranny, poverty, ignorance and ill health that characterized Egyptian life before the European intrusion; And, Egypt was forced in part by weapons but above all by the irresistible power of that revelation, to join the world capitalist market, for which Egypt was (and remains) poorly gifted.

This has been generally the case of the non-Western and marginal Western countries that can not ignore feeling, in that new situation of competition to which they were not accustomed, the discouragement of those who, having started late in a race, tend to notice their own advance less than the advantage of the leaders.

But there are not only disadvantages in being a late competitor.

Those who have entered the path to modernization late have at their disposal for free, or at a very low cost, the example and methods fashioned by the pioneers; the theory and practice of democracy; models and techniques of public and private administration that took centuries to initiate and perfect in the West; the accumulated and freely available scientific and technological knowledge; the evidence of co-piable successes and of avoidable errors in the adaptation of capitalism (or of socialism) for their own use; and above all, the very idea of the possibility of development instead of stagnation and of a reasonable welfare for the majority instead of extreme poverty, the first unsus-pected and the second presumed to be unreachable before the demon-stration of its feasibility by industrial, democratic, capitalistic society.

With respect to England, all of the other countries that have achieved a successful capitalist development were late competitors. One-hundred years ago ninety percent of the inhabitants of Sweden lived in conditions of extreme rural poverty. In the fifty years from 1860 to 1910, more than a million Swedes did not find any other way of escaping from that poverty than by emigrating to the United States. The backwardness of Germany in the first half of the nineteenth century was one of the reasons the young Marx became interested in economics.[9] In general, all the countries that are now advanced capital-ist countries were at one point at a disadvantage with relation to the surprising industrial, commercial, and military vigor of England. And all found that, in practice, the British advance, far from impeding their own take off, had opened the way for it. I say in practice, because in the realm of ideology, each one of these late competitors (not excluding the United States) in turn complained of the advance of England ("treacherous Albion") in terms similar to those that Third World propagandists use against capitalist civilization as a whole.

The requirements of this propaganda have caused the disparate grouping of the United States, Canada, and the most prosperous and balanced European countries, but also Italy and Spain, New Zealand, Australia, Israel, Japan (and probably soon Signapore, Hong Kong, Malaysia, South Korea, and Taiwan) in an "imperialist" bloc as heterogeneous and arbitrary as that supposedly made up by the so-called Third World. And that "imperialist" bloc will doubtless grow in the eyes of the Third World ideology by the addition of any number of late competitors who manage to break free not just from underdevelop-ment (a category applicable with greater justification to some so-called imperialist countries and most socialist countries) but also from the Third World ideology.

The Traumatic Stimulus

In synthesis, the global impact of capitalist civilization on the countries that are today classified as Third World (including both non-Western and marginal Western countries), but also on late competitors such as Germany, Sweden, Spain or Japan, can be characterized as a traumatic stimulus. Late competitors, Western, marginal Western or non-Western, have achieved uneven success in their reaction to that stimulus, but it is clear that the Third World ideology has been confounded: all of the late competitors without exception (including the socialist countries) have gained by the direct or indirect efforts of the development first in Great Britain and later in the rest of Western Europe and the United States of the surprising phenomenon that has been capitalist civilization.

Even the poorest and most backward of the late competitors find themselves much better off today than before the unsettling of their stagnation by the impact of capitalism; better off in measurable indexes of economic growth, public health, education, consumption; and better off in something not measurable but essential: their spiritual tone, the condition of being awake, alert and demanding. There is a vast difference for the better between present-day Arabs and those described by Renan a hundred years ago, sleeping like lizards among the ruins of Petra and Palmyra, making him exclaim: "Damned are people without wants!"[10]

There was a time, less disoriented than ours, when this seemed what in truth it is—totally obvious. Then the greatest hope of non-Western countries was clearly perceived as residing in the impact of the West on peoples that were either primitive, or succesors of great civilizations in decline and which, even at their height had been despotic, slave-based societies, indifferent to suffering and inequality and incapable of suspecting what immense productive forces could be released by the ingenuity of free men pursuing their private interest within a free society.

Marxism and Third World Ideology

In all the writings of Karl Marx and Frederick Engels there is not a single reference to the relations of dominance and dependence as a supposed explanation for the advance of European countries and of the United States, or as supposed related cause of the backwardness of Africa, Asia and Latin America. There is not a trace in Marx and

Engels of what I have called the Third World ideology, today central to the socialist discourse. According to the ideology, the advanced capitalist nations have achieved their prosperity and the countries of the Third World their poverty, principally due to the links of domination and dependence that join them, so that simply by breaking these links—making the revolution—any Third World country could overcome as if by magic its secular problems and enter into a rapid path to prosperity, justice and liberty.

Rather, there are numerous texts by Marx and Engels that in a clear and even explicit way contradict the Third World ideology; and this in spite of the fact that Marx lived until 1883, and Engels until 1895. They therefore had all the information used by Hobson (1902) and Lenin (1916) to propose the basis of the ideology and the bulk of the arguments that from then on have been mouthed by successive generations of Third World ideologists.

The British presence in India dates from the sixteenth century, and turned into absolute domination even before Marx was born (1818). The Dutch arrived in Java (Indonesia) in the seventeenth century. The Spaniards conquered what is now called Spanish America and also the Phillipine Islands before 1600. France had influence in Indochina from the sixteenth century on, and made the peninsula a colony in 1858. The same France conquered Algeria in 1830, when Engels was ten years old. In 1853 the Americans forced Japan to begin a process of integration into the world capitalist market. Chinese resistance to the same process was broken by the English in the so-called Opium War of 1842. Ceylon had been a British colony since 1796; West Africa since 1838. Egypt was converted into a British protectorate in 1882, one year before the death of Marx and thirteen years before the death of Engels. The Belgians colonized the Congo between 1876 and 1885 and the war and annexation of Mexican territory by the United States took place between 1846 and 1848.

In addition, by 1848, when Marx and Engels were thirty and twenty-eight years old respectively and had already written the *Communist Manifesto,* the imperialist countries (that according to the theory of dependence, supposedly owe their progress to the backwardness of the Third World, and vice versa) had all achieved manifest levels of advantage in their economic, political, social, scientific, and technological development over the rest of the world. So in 1848, the imperialist impact of the West on the Third World had already taken place, with full evidence of all its good and bad consequences for both parties; furthermore the differences between nations were if anything more marked then than they are now. Nevertheless, the "first thinker of the century" (Engels in a speech before Karl Marx's tomb) did not once hint that the development of the advanced countries and the backwardness of the Asian, African, and Latin American countries could in the least be explained by that imperialist impact. On the contrary, he saw it to be clearly the only promise of progress for the areas of the globe that today we call the Third World.

And Engels, in a text as late as his prologue to the 1893 reissue of *The Condition of the Working Class in England,* insists more than ever on the importance of colonial expansion for palliating the crises of overproduction of the advanced capitalist economies. He did not dream of putting the cart before the horse and suggest, against all evidence and logic, that the industrial advance (the cause of that superproduction) of England, France, Holland, and Belgium (the imperialist countries par excellence) was due in the first place to the fact that they possessed colonies; nor did he suggest that countries without colonies and without overseas influence of any kind, such as Austria, Germany, Denmark, and Switzerland owed anything to a second degree participation in who knows what mysterious advantages supposedly derived from their intrinsically "imperialist" nature.

The expectations of Marx and many other nineteenth-century humanitarians about the modernizing influence of the West on the non-Western or marginal Western countries were perhaps too optimistic. In our eyes there seems to be a naive confidence on the part of Marx and his epoch in the invincible force of capitalist progress once it was geared into action. We think we know better than Marx, because in the short term development has lagged behind newly felt needs. But this shouldn't make us lose sight of the fact that in relation with the levels of development of both the non-Western countries before their contact with the capitalist West, and of the Western countries themselves before their capitalist development, the so-called Third World today enjoys (except in cases of special misfortune in no way imputable to the West) levels of life, education, health and consumption without precedent before capitalism entered mankind's experience.[11]

The Alteration of the Equilibrium of Poverty

Because it is so easily demonstrated, this point is not denied by all the critics of capitalist civilization. Some of them make a tactical retreat and reestablish their positions on the basis of the argument that the West (imperialism) is at the very least responsible for having caused disruptions in certain historic equilibria that existed before its expansion.

John Kenneth Galbraith[12], for example, points out how in the nineteenth century the English built vast irrigation systems to compensate for irregular rainfall in Northern India (This improved extension of land is still today the largest area with artificial irrigation in the world). As a complementary measure, railroads were built that permitted a better and more just (in the words of Galbraith) distribution of the additional food resources thus obtained. A large part of the railway network built by the British colonial administration was designed principally to combat the traditional cycles of famine. The immense resources invested in the realization of these projects were not contributed, with the exception of labor (paid, of course) by the local population. Without question, we are in the presence of an admirable scheme destined to improve the living standards of millions of human beings.

Galbraith's argument continues to say that the net result of this disruption in the previously existing "equilibrium of poverty" was the survival of masses that without that intromission would have died or would not have been born. As a result, the new resources were very soon spread among a much greater number of people, all of them as poor as before.

If that has been the result of Western initiatives that must be recognized as philanthropic, what can be expected of the distortions in the social fabric of the Third World caused by the greediness of transnational capitalism?

In New York in 1979 I watched on television some American communists who vehemently argued that the then recent holding of American diplomatic hostages by Iran was fully justified, because they claimed the United States had created the miserable slums of Teheran. Pressed by the interviewer to support such an affirmation, they offered the usual answer: before oil, Iran was supposedly a harmonious and happy society; its population was stable; its cities were models of rational urbanism.

Each one of these assertions is false, or refers, idealizing it, to a deplorable former reality of deep poverty and great unhappiness. The only affirmation that is true is the argument with regard to the previous stability of the population. In fact, before capitalist civilization, the ubiquitous combination of a dreadful infant mortality and a very short life expectancy for the survivors resulted in an almost universal stability of populations precariously clinging to the edge of what Galbraith calls the equilibrium of poverty. The changes in those societies caused by the impact of the West resulted in a dramatic decline of infant mortality and in an equally spectacular increase in general life expectancy. The consequence, in societies that were poor to begin with, is that there are many more poor people, in absolute numbers.

Even though this is a serious problem, it does not follow that it has replaced a better situation. Far from being an iniquity perpetrated by capitalism against the Third World, it actually reflects a remarkable improvement in the living standards of those populations. Those who survive have been, without the slightest doubt, better off than those who died from starvation or disease; and those survivors would little appreciate the Third World ideology's claim that their existence and that of their children is the result of harm that the West has maliciously perpetrated on the societies to which they belong.

It is a sign of the dishonesty, or at least of the flippancy of those who brandish this argument, that they themselves do not hesitate to turn it inside out, like a glove, when measures (other Western sanitary technologies) are proposed to counteract, through birth control, the effects of the previous "imperialist" introduction of the prophylactic, therapeutic, agricultural and industrial techniques that originally caused the explosive growth of the population, increasing the absolute number of those suffering from poverty. Population control is in turn described as genocide, and it is judged as destined not to palliate the same runaway demographic growth that on the other hand is de-nounced as a misfortune caused by capitalism, but rather as a selfish scheme, inspired solely by the fear of the rich countries before the large and growing population of the poor countries.

The True "Western Malaise"

P. T. Bauer shows[13] that there is a way in which the West has undoubtedly contributed to the economic and political difficulties of the Third World, not with the usual recriminations, but with one that is never made. It is the politization of all the economic and social life of those countries, the atrophy or the destruction in them of civil society, by the innoculation of their elites with the virulent socialist illusion about the intrinsic virtue of state control and therefore of all extensions of the jurisdiction and powers of governments.

In the last years of the British imperial domination, when Great Britain had a socialist government, the Asian, African, and Antillean English colonies had bestowed upon then sundry measures favoring state control, such as the establishment of government monopolies in the export trade. More generally, a government structure favoring the growth of state control was one of the legacies that the new states received, as successors of the British colonial administration, and this coincided perfectly and unfortunately with the personal inclinations of the native leaders of the nascent Third World.[14]

Daniel P. Moynihan[15] has shown how and where those leaders acquired such inclinations. He recalls that most of the new states that received their independence from 1947, rapidly raising the number of members of the United Nations from 51 to almost 150, had (and maintain) within a great diversity, a common feature: their native leaders "shared the general body of British socialist animus, such as developed between 1890 and 1950, approximately." The general features of that British socialist animus are the following: the substitution of private property in all possible cases, and eventually in all essential areas of the economy; the substitution of production for profit by production for use; the substitution of competition by cooperation; the substitution of "personal selfish interest" by collective and altruistic interest; the regulation of all areas of economic activity not under direct state control; and planning.

This British doctrinary socialist animus is contemptuous of economic growth, which it considers vulgar and moreover unnecessary. Its belief, already from the end of the nineteenth century, is that there exists sufficient wealth, only that it us unfairly distributed. Its central message then, is the necessity of the redistribution of income, not its growth. Even in the cases of evident generalized poverty, what happens is that wealth is hidden by the capitalists, or (in the case of the peripheries of capitalism) is drained toward the metropolis. This last mentioned is the central argument of the Third World ideology.

What was involved, then, was not solely that the British labor government would rapidly put into operation after 1945, and bequeath to the new states, interventionist and state-controlled administrative structures, but rather, much more important, that the leaders of those new states, from their days as students in Great Britain, were drenched in the ideology corresponding to those structures.

Here there is indeed a grave harm done by the West to the countries of the Third World. Instead of transmitting to them steam for capitalist civilization, it contaminated them with paralyzing anticapitalist prejudices. "The poorer a country is, the poorer will be its administrative resources (the only exception may be China, a totally special case). Therefore, it is pathetic to attempt in those countries a system of social organization as complicated as socialism, and more so in its form of extreme statism. Poor societies should attempt that liberation of the initiative and energy of individuals in which Adam Smith and Karl Marx coincided in seeing the key to the primitive economic take-off. But in the intellectual and political climate of our time, there are not many leaders in the poor countries ready to recognize such an apparently conservative truth."[16]

From 1917 on, the communist ideology, as it was defined by the theories and practices of Lenin and his successors in the Soviet Union and other Soviet-type states, has made an enormous contribution to the anticapitalist intellectual and political climate of our times. But the terrain had been fertilized by the West, and particularly by the British socialists, including John Atkinson Hobson. In his book *Imperialism* (1902), he stated the essential tenets that Lenin would later popularize in his *Imperialism, Supreme Stage of Capitalism* (1917) and that have permeated all political discourse in the form of what I have called the Third World ideology.

Within the terms of that ideology, the only recrimination that will never be made to the West is the one that would have the greatest justification: having furnished to the leaders of the emerging Third World the socialist animus, ready for consumption. And of course they have avidly swallowed it, because socialism leads straight to greater power for those who are in government, and to absolute power when the socialism practiced is of the "perfect" variety, that is to say, totalitarian.

The economic consequences of this devotion of the leaders of the Third World to some form of socialism or to the sum of fallacies of the Third World ideology have been catastrophic. Nothing is simple, and nothing has a single explanation. Nevertheless, the fact must have some meaning that in 1947, the year of its independence, India produced 1,200,000 tons of steel per year, and Japan scarcely 900,000; and that a mere quarter of a century later (in 1972) the respective figures were 6,800,000 and 106,800,000. Moynihan argues[17] with reason that the different result was essentially due to divergent decisions taken after 1947 by the political leaders of those two countries.[18] It is perfectly conceivable that if Japan had been a British colony before 1947, its political leaders also would have insisted that a "basic industry" of "strategic significance" such as steel should be developed by the public sector, as in India, with results that might have been deplorable and for once entirely attributable to the nefarious influence of imperialism and colonialism.

Notes

1. About the theory of unequal exchanges, see Emmanuel Arghiri, *L'Echange Inégal. Un essai sur les antagonismes dans les rapports internationaux (présentation et rémarques théoriques de Charles Bettelheim)*

(Paris: Maspéro, 1969). And for a refutation of that theory, see Paul A. Samuelson, "Illogisme de la doctrine néo-marxienne de l'échange inégal" and Pascal Salin, "Echange inégal et illusion scientifique." The latter appeared in *Commentaire,* Paris, no. 17, Spring 1982.

2. For example, at the summit of nonaligned countries, in Havana, 1979, Manley said: "The antiimperialist forces in our hemisphere are today more vigorous than ever because our hemisphere has had a movement and a man, a catalyst and a rock. The catalyst has been the Cuban revolution, and the man is Fidel Castro."

3. As is known, Manley lost the election of 30 October 1980. The new prime minister of Jamaica, Edward Seaga, expressly rejects the Third World ideology. His first act of government was to expel the Cuban Ambassador whose intromission in the internal affairs of Jamaica had been scandalous.

4. Carlos Alberto Montaner, *Secret Report on the Cuban Revolution* (New Brunswick, N.J.: Transaction, 1981). It is worth recalling that in 1959 Cuba ranked third in per capita income in Latin America.

5. Ibid.

6. Only considerable ecomomic success could have persuaded Chile to put up with the political abuses of the Popular Unity government, but the Allende administration proved utterly inept in economic matters. When Frei left the presidency, Chile was standing by all its international obligations; it had accumulated reserves amounting to $500 million—an unprecedented figure; during the last two years of Frei's mandate, the country had contracted no foreign debts other than those destined for capital investment. When it was learned that the Christian Democrats would cast their votes for Allende in the final congressional vote for the presidency, the economic situation immediately took a turn for the worse. And responsibility for this ecomomic deterioration, which began even before Allende's inauguration, lies with Popular Unity; this was the natural reaction of a free enterprise system that had just learned it would soon be cornered and throttled by an incoming government.

   Allende's first ecomomic measures included a general wage increase, the freezing of prices, the settling of an unrealistically high fixed official rate of exchange for the national currency, and a considerable increase in public expenditures, largely invested in the acquisition of private enterprises. The appropriation of private businesses was carried out at a steady pace through a variety of means. The stock market panicked, so that the government was able to acquire control of many corporations by buying up their shares at nominal cost. Other corporations, whose shares were not quoted on the stock market, were disrupted by endless strikes, which were organized to justify the state's interference on the basis of reactivating production. Agriculture experienced the same kind of strangulation as private industrial activity. As was to be expected, the copper mines, which represented practically the single source of foreign exchange, were expropriated; the state took over the 49 percent of the stock still in foreign hands, and assumed direct control over their administration.

   These measures led to a sudden rise in the purchasing of consumer goods, both domestic and imported, at artificially low prices, which were in fact subsidized by the state through the arbitrarily high rate of the Chilean escudo, supported by a hemorrhage of foreign-currency reserves. Naturally, this at first created a feeling of euphoria; productivity remained low, but employment figures and production rose temporarily. The real purchasing power of salaries rose by nearly 30 percent.

But this mini-boom during the first months of 1971 reflected only the dissipation of reserves, the spending of wealth built up in previous years. During the second half of the year, the discrepancy between production costs and prices, further compounded by the stagnation or actual decline of production in industry, agriculture, and cattle breeding, inevitably resulted in shortages and in the development of a black market. In 1970, the last year of the Frei administration, Chile had had a positive balance of payments of 91 million dollars; in 1971, there was a deficit of 315 million dollars. In November 1971, after a year of the Allende administration, Chile had to declare itself insolvent and asked for a moratorium on its foreign debts. One month later, the artificial value of the escudo began to crumble: the Central Bank of Chile could no longer support the national currency. In one year, the government had doubled the amount of paper currency in circulation to finance its programs. Private investments, national and foreign, had fallen to zero. The state had invested its assets mostly in nationalizing existing sectors of production; it had added practically no new sources of production to the economy. A majority of the professional and highly skilled members of society were by now shaken and demoralized; a large number were in opposition to government. Many chose to emigrate (26 percent of the country's engineers, for example). (Carlos Rangel, *The Latin Americans: Their Love-Hate Relationship with the United States* [New York: Harcourt Brace Jovanovich, 1977], pp. 267-72.)

7. The brain drain is produced not only by socialist Third World experiments, such as those of Manley and Allende, or by communist dictatorships, or by Third World tyrannies such as that of Idi Amin Dada in Uganda. The phenomenon occurs every time that for some reason living conditions become unbearable for those who feel themselves compelled to emigrate, or to flee, or are expelled. The military dictatorships of Paraguay and Uruguay have produced a brain drain. Other examples of the escape, expulsion or destruction of educated minorities include the expulsion of the Jews and Moslems by Spain in the fifteenth century, the revocation of the Edict of Nantes by Louis XIV, and the destruction of the European Jews by Hitler. Neither Spain, France, nor the whole of Europe have entirely recovered from these self-inflicted wounds.

8. I owe this information to the circumstance of having read the Doctoral Dissertation of the Venezuelan sociologist, Sara Natalia Meneses Imber, presented to Stanford University, and entitled *Scholarship Programs as Mechanisms of Socio-cultural Incorporation into Transnational Capitalism: A Case Study of the Venezuelan Government Foundation "Gran Mariscal de Ayacucho."*

9. Engels emphasized the importance, for the development of socialist movements, of developed bourgeois conditions, "which in Germany, after

the wars of the Reformation and the Peasant Wars, particularly after the Thirty Years' War, could not arise for centuries. The separation of Holland from the Empire forced Germany out of world trade and from the outset reduced its industrial development to the scantiest proportions; and while the Germans were so slowly and laboriously recovering from the devastation of the civil wars, while they were using up all their civil energy, which had never been very great, in fruitless struggle against the customs barriers and idiotic trade regulations which every petty princeling and imperial baron imposed on the industry of his subjects, while the imperial towns with their guild mummery and patrician hauteur were falling into decay, Holland, England and France conquered the leading positions in world trade, founded colony after colony and developed the manufacturing industry to the highest pitch of prosperity, until finally England, owing to steam power which only then began to impart value to its coal and iron deposits, attained the foremost position in modern bourgeois development. (Frederick Engels, "Karl Marx, A Contribution to the Critique of Political Economy," in Karl Marx and Frederick Engels, *Selected Works,* vol. 1 [Moscow: Foreign Languages Publishing House, 1951], p. 332).

10. "The misery of being exploited by capitalists is nothing compared to the misery of not being exploited at all." Joan Robinson, *Economic Philosophy* (Garden City, N.Y.: Doubleday, 1964), p. 45, quoted in John Kenneth Galbraith, *The Nature of Mass Poverty* (Cambridge: Harvard University Press, 1979) p. 91n.

11. The preindustrial countries are in the condition one might think of as historically "normal." Many people—Kenneth Boulding, Peter Drucker, J. M. Keynes, for example—have pointed out that for the last ten thousand years or so, excluding the last two or three centuries, no large human society has ever produced more than the equivalent of some $200 per capita per year, nor dropped much below about $50 per capita per year for any appreciable period of time. Kenneth Boulding points out that, from this point of view, Indonesia represents "normal civilization"—or "civilization"—since it has a population of some 100 million people, roughly that of the Han Empire or the Roman Empire, and an average per capita income of about $100 per year. Thus most Indonesians live in a manner recognizable to both the Romans and the Han Chinese, and "if Indonesians could visit such economies, they would find much that is familiar." Quoted by Herman Kahn and Anthony J. Wiener, *The Year 2000* (New York: Macmillan, 1967), p. 57.

12. Galbraith, *The Nature of Mass Poverty,* pp. 56-57.

13. In several of his works. For example, in "Western Guilt and Third World Poverty," *Commentary* (January 1976): 31-38. Professor Bauer (of the London School of Economics) is one of the few courageous voices that have dared defy the mass of falsities and half truths produced by the Third World ideology and its hand maiden, the so-called development literature. His fundamental book on these themes is justly called *Dissent on Development,* (London: Weidenfeld & Nicholson, 1971). Other relevant works by Bauer are: *The Ecomomics of Underdeveloped Countries* (with B. S. Yamey, also of the London School of Economics); *Economic Analysis and Policy in Underdeveloped Countries; Indian Economic Policy and Devel-*

opment; Equality, The Third World and Economic Delusion. "Against the New Economic Order," *Commentary* (April 1977).

14. Of the new states that have entered the United Nations since 1947, nearly fifty were part of the British Empire before their independence. The Third World is composed in large part of former British colonies.

15. Daniel Patrick Moynihan, "The United States in Opposition," *Commentary* (March 1975): 31-44.

16. John Kenneth Galbraith, *Le Temps des incertitudes* (Paris: Gallimard, 1978), p. 390.

17. Moynihan, in the above quoted article.

18. And he adds: "Who, having read British political journals over the past quarter century, would be surprised to find that during this period (1950-1973) the United Kingdom's share of the 'Planetary Product' has been reduced from 5.8 to 3.1 percent? Why then be surprised that those who have made British socialism their model have trouble taking off in the opposite direction?" (Moynihan, in the above quoted article, p. 39).

5

The Capitalist Revolution

The fact that the West has derived important advantages from its relations with what is today known as the Third World is not under discussion. Imperialism and the exploitation of weak by strong countries are historical constants. Powerful human groups have always defeated and conquered weaker human groups and have perpetrated abuses, extortions, and humiliations upon them. What is false is to hold that the imperial powers known throughout history have derived their power from those extortions, which obviously could take place only because decisive differences in power existed before all contact, before all unjust transference of the wealth of the weak to the strong.

Besides, it is not enough that a power have the capacity of foreign imperial action in order to really benefit from that transfer of wealth. The example of Spain, ruined by its fantastic imperialist success in the Americas, is sufficient to show that the greatest transfer of wealth can even be harmful, if the society that receives it does not have as well a capacity for internal action much more important and decisive for its own prosperity and social balance than the capacity for external military action that permits it to conquer other countries.

Furthermore, the most inflated estimate of the imperial advantages enjoyed by Western countries that have besides achieved an advanced capitalist development, cannot begin to explain even a small fraction of their accumulated wealth since the capitalist industrial revolution up to the present time. Much more merciless relations of domination had existed before in history without having produced anything remotely similar to the fantastic ecomomic expansion of the West in modern times. It was because of the wealth and technological advance that it had previously generated that the West was capable, as an effect and not as a cause, to politically, economically, and culturally dominate the rest of the world for such a long time. The erosion of that domination in our time is, on the other hand, the demonstration that non-Western and marginal Western countries, previously defenseless, far from having been overwhelmed and ruined by the traumatic stimulus of Western imperialism, have pulled themselves up to levels of vigor and expectations to which they would not have aspired had they not received that stimulus. The future will perhaps find premature the idea that Marx overestimated the positive aspects of the impact of advanced Western capitalism on the static cultures of Asia and Africa and on the marginal Western countries, such as the Iberian and Latin American countries.

Colonialism: a Bad Business

Some of the most dynamic Western countries never had colonies or even any indirect form of domination over any of the territories today called Third World. This is true of Switzerland, Sweden, Norway, Denmark, and Austria. Others were themselves colonies. This is true of the United States, Canada, Australia, and New Zealand. The three last mentioned countries, far from having exerted domination over anyone, today remain closely dependent with relation to other capitalist countries of much greater economic dimensions; so, according to that indispensable prop of the Third World ideology, the dependency theory, the drag of Great Britain on those countries (or the drag of the United States on Canada) should have frustrated them at least as much as is said to be true (because of dependency) of Mexico and Argentina.

Both Germany and Japan tried and ephemerally achieved the construction of colonial empires; but, defeated in wars and despoiled of their conquests, they have remained since 1945 not only deprived of all domination over other countries, but had to start in that year from zero or worse. They had been devastated, occupied, amputated. Nevertheless, due to their intrinsic qualities and to the wise adoption starting then of a market economy worthy of that name, they achieved their greatest economic growth right after having suffered catastrophes comparable or worse than almost any other in history.

Great Britain, owner for a century of the greatest empire, saw the loss of its colonies coincide with a persistent economic decline, which could suggest a cause-and-effect relation between the privileges of the colonialist metropolis and its former rise and present decadence. But the very different experience of Belgium, France, and Holland suggests that one must search elsewhere for the root of Great Britain's difficulties. Perhaps they stem from the perverse effect on the economy of that "corpus of British socialist thought" of which Moynihan speaks, whose full impact was wrought upon the British economy starting right from the Labor Party's electoral victory in 1945.

In their colonies, the imperial countries dissipated enormous resources in military, bureaucratic and other unprofitable expenses which, as nations, they did not recuperate. For example, Belgium's King Leopold II extracted an enormous personal fortune from the Belgian Congo, because the costs of the colonial adventure were paid by the whole Belgian nation, while only Leopold drew profits. From a strictly economic point of view, both Belgium and its king would have benefited from an arrangement by which the country would have directly transferred a fraction of the cost of the conquest and colonization of the Congo to Leopold. The king would have had more profits, Belgium fewer expenditures, and this without a single Belgian citizen having to move to Africa and act there as protagonist of such sordid and terrible adventures as those described by Conrad in *Heart of Darkness*.

In other colonial metropolises there was a multiplicity of Leopolds, but the basic equation was similar: profits for a few, a considerably higher cost than those profits for the nation. Otherwise, how can we explain that Holland and Belgium had the greatest expansion and prosperity of their history precisely after losing their colonies?

The case of France is still more remarkable. Legitimate French businesses (distinct from the traffic in money or drugs) in Indochina, Madagascar, and North Africa, were ruined after 1945 because of the wars made necessary by the French effort to maintain its domination over those territories. Therefore France ceased deriving the flimsiest profit from its colonies, and at the same time saw its burden thereof tremendously increased in the vain effort to stop decolonization. Yet not even that clear drag could impede the formidable and entirely domestic fueled postwar French economic expansion.

It is worth emphasizing that there was a European country, or rather two, that actually turned themselves into parasites of their colonies. And the poor economic performance of Spain and Portugal in the modern world, in comparison with territories and populations which one of them dominated and exploited in the sixteenth and seventeenth centuries in the fullest meaning of those terms—the Netherlands and Lombardy—is sufficient proof of the emptiness of the Third World thesis on the ineluctable correlation between colonial domination and development on the one hand and dependency and backwardness on the other. Spain and Portugal, advanced in the area of naval power in the fifteenth century compared to the rest of Europe, in a few years seized vast colonies that were held by Spain for three centuries and by Portugal, with the exception of Brazil, until recently. But deprived of the social virtues (vices, according to the Third World ideology) that generated and sustained the modernization of other Western countries, the two Iberian powers squandered the product of the exploitation of their colonies in luxury, leisure, arrogance; and also in the freezing of their social structures by coercion, subsidized obscurantism, bribes and handouts to the unemployed. It was excess wealth, unearned and used in a noncapitalistic manner which set back Spain and Portugal and cornered them into a marginal position in relation to those Western countries whose take-off to modernization anteceded any American, African, or Asian conquest.

The Vindication of Tyrants

Such unquestionable facts should by themselves dissipate at least one of the two pillars of the Third World ideology. It would be possible to go on arguing until disproved, that the countries today called Third World had been arrested in their development because of their relation to the imperial capitalist countries, but hardly that the latter owe their prosperity solely or at least essentially to their advantages as imperial powers.

But the purpose of socialist propaganda in its Third World ideology form is not to reach scientific truths, but to mask or muddle even the most obvious conclusions that should be impossible not to infer from commonsense analysis of easily obtained information. This is achieved by the exploitation of emotions and prejudices through a dialectical pirouette enormously appreciated by the public to which it is destined, and which consists of holding that imperialism need not be a question of direct political domination, or of brutal plundering, but that it can function as well (or better) through a subtle network of economic, political, and cultural relations. Thus it can be advanced that Sweden and Switzerland owe their prosperity and progress to imperialism no less than Great Britain, France, Belgium or Holland, and in the same breath that Third World countries would have long since shaken off backwardness and poverty, *or they wouldn't ever have suffered them,* if it had not been for their dependent insertion in the world capitalist system.

A very revealing and characteristic aspect of this imaginary explanation (pleasing and therefore popular among the peoples to whom it is directed) of the differences in power, prosperity, and social progress between the distinct nation-states on today's world scene, is the current exaltation of any despot who in his time tried to stop or slow down the insertion of his country in the capitalist order, not because of any nationalist clairvoyance dishonestly and antihistorically attributed to this type of ruler, but rather for strictly obscurantist reasons, such as religious fanaticism, xenophobia, or the astute and vile calculation that it is easier to keep tyrannical social control over a population if it lacks information about the world outside.

A case in point is that of the Paraguayan dictator Gaspar Rodriguez Francia (1814-1840) and his immediate successors, the Lopezes, father (1840-63) and son (1863-70). For a long time it was universally agreed that these three tyrants not only martyrized the Paraguayan people with implacable repression and obscurantism, but that the last of them literally led Paraguay to destruction: in an insane war against Brazil, Argentina, and Uruguay (1864-70) led by the second Lopez in an entirely characteristic way, until almost the whole adult and adolescent male population of Paraguay died in combat.

This Paraguayan national tragedy has been turned in recent years into the following fable: The acknowledgedly autocratic (how can it be denied?) governments of Gaspar Rodriguez Francia and the two Lopezes had the "virtue" of accentuating the isolation of Paraguay,[1] whose contacts abroad were in any case precarious due to the Argentinian and Uruguayan control of the mouth of the River Plate. That isolation soon made Paraguay "a self-sufficient nation, supported on small agricultural property and thriving hand crafts."[2] On this "natural" economy, "premonetary in its principal productive branches" (A pointed allusion to that abolition of the monetary economy that is one of the principal theoretical elements of the socialist utopia) and "by the official control" of all exports and "the closing of the country to international trade and finance, the two Lopezes consolidated a state policy that transformed Paraguay into an island of economic autonomy and political self-determination in Latin America."

What follows is truly astonishing: "Drawing advantages from its isolation [sic],[3] Paraguay constructed railroads and telegraph lines, foundries, shipyards, factories capable of producing agricultural implements, weapons, munitions, textiles and paper." And the fiction does not stop there: "On this infrastructure, an army was organized that in 1865 was probably one of the best in South America. In time of peace soldiers were busy in such civil projects as construction of railways, irrigation channels, bridges, roads and laying down telegraph lines, in addition to state industries and public works. It is said that (the second) Lopez taught to read and write almost the whole Paraguayan population . . .".

One wonders how this accumulation of miracles had been ignored not only in Latin American historiography, but also in world historiography, so lacking in examples of happiness of a people stemming from the beneficent action of virtuous and wise princes. The explanation will have to be found in the perversity of liberal historiography, which invested all its labors in presenting as praiseworthy the misdeeds of Miranda, Bolívar, Andres Bello, Mitre, Sarmiento, and Juarez, while it slandered or ignored the authentic heroes of Latin America, Gaspar Rodriguez Francia, Antonio Carlos Lopez, Francisco Solano Lopez, Rosas (Argentina) Belzu (Bolivia) and other similar figures.

Where fable becomes frightful reality is in the following: "[The second Lopez] inflamed the national [Paraguayan] valor, transforming the people [in a year, two years, in five?] into a *Herrenvolk* [sic] disposed to expand beyond its frontiers with Brazil and Argentina and reach larger territorial dimensions. Paraguay hurls itself into a war against Brazil. . . . It fought alone, because Argentina and Uruguay took Brazil's side. The Paraguayan people were crushed."[4]

Before that insane war Paraguay had about one-and-a-half million inhabitants. After, there remained (according to an 1871 census) scarcely 221,079, distributed in the following way: 28,746 elderly or invalid, 106,254 women, and 86,079 children. This does not stop the author whom we have been quoting from stating that under Francia and the Lopezes, Paraguay was "an experiment demonstrative of the potentiality of the neo-American protoethnia, of what the *new peoples* of Latin America could achieve if they were led in an autonomus direction"; and also that "after the colonial period, there followed (in Paraguay) a stage of isolation with regard to the imperialist European expansion that did not mean poverty and backwardness, but exactly the opposite: technical and economic progress and cultural development. The civilizing capacity of the neoguarani, of the ladino, of the gaucho, as well as that of the Venezuelan llanero, of the cholo from the Andean altiplano, of the Mexican cepero, of the Ecuadorean montuvio, of the Chilean huaso, and of the neo-Brazilian, was proved [sic] (in Paraguay) with an eloquence that would not be repeated until our days."[5]

Where Left and Right Meet

A recent book written by an American professor[6] is entirely devoted to arguing that the obscurantist tyrants are the true (although slandered) heroes of Latin American history, and the only rulers who have been in tune with the masses, only to be frustrated by the pro-European and modernizing liberals and by imperialism. He refers to Francia and the two Lopezes in Paraguay, Rosas in Argentina, and Belzu in Bolivia. What leads the good American professor to exalt Belzu, one of the most grotesque and brutal tyrants that Latin America has endured? Surely the socialist rhetoric of this dictator is quoted admiringly and without noticing that these words, spoken in 1850 in the Bolivian high plateau, were as Western as the railroads Belzu is implicitly praised for not building. He said, for example: "Friends: private property is the source [of all the evils] of Bolivia. In the words of a great philosopher: private property is the result of the exploitation of the weak by the strong. Down with private property! Down with property owners! We have had enough of exploitation of man by his fellow man."[7]

Treading even deeper water, the Latin American Marxist left has begun to exalt Lope de Aguirre as an admirable libertarian. Aguirre was a member of the expedition sent in 1560 by the Viceroy of Peru to explore the Amazon from its source in the eastern slopes of the Peruvian Andes. The man, who clearly was a psychopathic killer, managed in two bloody episodes to take over command of the expedition. At times killing his own men and always any others who crossed his path, he reached Venezuela, where tradition has recorded for him the epithet of "The Tyrant."[8]

He has always been acknowledged as a fascinating personality because of his uncommon bloody cruelty and his boldness and rebelliousness. He is supposed to have sent a letter to Phillip II declaring as dissolved the relation of vassalage between him and the King. Spanish and Latin American historians and novelists have always been struck by this man, but without dreaming to suggest what is said from the title of a recent novel by a Venezuelan communist writer: *Lope de Aguirre, Prince of Liberty.* [9]

It is somewhere between amusing and dismaying to find in conservative or simply mercenary literature written in praise of Latin American tyrants, arguments in every respect similar to those that are now fashionable in the Third World ideology. For example, during the life of the implacable Venezuelan dictator Juan Vicente Gomez, (1908-1935) and probably at his expense, the Colombian writer Fernando Gonzalez published a panegyric of Gomez entitled *Mi Compadre*[10]. (Gomez was godfather of one of Gonzalez's sons). Gonzalez constructs an apology for the "telluric" dictator on the basis of Amerindian ethnicity, and this with more logic than those who, for tactical reasons, systematically forget that blacks in America are as unauthoctonous as whites. "My hope in [Latin America]," writes Gonzalez, "lies on its Indian blood." Why hasn't Latin America found its direction and its destiny? Because, until Gomez arises in Venezuela, "whites and mulattos have governed with European ideas and methods . . .". Over and over again Gonzalez returns to his topic: a man functions only when he is connected by blood to telluric forces. A white is out of joint in Latin America, but also a black or a mulatto. This alien blood will be integrated only with difficulty and the passing of time, when the descendants of whites and blacks have incorported a sufficient portion of Amerindian blood. "[The Amerindian blood] is acclimated. It possesses the wisdom of our continent." Gomez "has not travelled abroad, nor is he spoiled by [a foreign oriented] education."[11] He is "the son of Indian chiefs," he is "a racial agent at the service of the destinies of South America." It is true that he is the victim of a propaganda campaign, calling him barbarian and tyrant. But see who the slanderers are: spiritual vassals of European liberalism,[12] who understand nothing of the Latin American essence. Against them Gonzalez has (or feigns) only contempt. On the other hand, Gomez inspires him to this invocation: "Fathers of South America, Indian chiefs, masters of our rivers, who know how to gather fish without violence . . . who know how to ford the great rivers. Silent Indians who instantly grasped the meaning that issues from the eyes and from the whole human body, to guess hidden intentions . . . Silent and suffering Indians who knew how to cure with the plants of South America, who softened gold, who heard the distant noises in the forest . . . Fathers who were one with this land as the pulp of the coconut is to its shell: free me from the mulattoes and the whites who do not know whence they came nor where they are going. Free me from them, who use things that they have not made . . . From them nothing has sprung, and they have given nothing to South American life . . . I invoke your blood, Indian fathers. In Venezuela (with Gomez) there is a new dawn."

Except for the style, there is deep agreement between Gonzalez and the newly sprung leftist apologists of traditional tyrants inspired by a militant left wing anthropology now in fashion. Myths by definition die hard, and if yesterday they were brandished by the ultraconservative right, today they can be useful for the ultraradical left.

Genuine Autarchy

The left's current exaltation of the obscurantist tyrants that Latin America has endured, and the corresponding denigration of liberal modernizing rulers, is meant to promote the socialist theory that liberal modernization (capitalism) ruined Latin America. The liberal modernizers (of whom the Argentinian Sarmiento is the paradigm) supposedly have caused untold harm by their efforts to fully incorporate Latin America into the West. The reactionaries (such as Gaspar Rodriguez Francia) must be praised and admired for having blocked modernization and for having kept the people they tyranized in a condition of supposedly beneficent autarchy; and this, obviously, because thus they hindered for a while the establishment of links of dependence with the centers of world capitalism.

This idealization of Latin American autarchy is patently absurd. Latin America is not "Westernized," it is essentially Western, as much as the United States or Canada. It is therefore fraudulent to pretend that Latin America has ever had the option of accepting or rejecting Western civilization, or that the latter has been an exotic import of the modernizers.

Now, just for the sake of pursuing the argument for autarchy and the rejection of Western influence and seeing where it leads, let us observe that there are in the world a few cases of genuine autarchy with relation to the capitalist industrial revolution, where the sheer topography, or the absence of incentives to conquest and colonization, or both factors together kept some nations isolated from the traumatic stimulus of contact with the West. In this way, some of the most backward nations of the world were never colonized or established significant commerical and cultural bonds with the West.

A case of almost perfect purity in autarchy, and therefore exemplary, is offered by Ethiopia, a nation in whose life foreign influences, especially those of the modern West, were absent to the greatest possible degree.[13] Just a few Europeans, explorers for the sources of the Nile or eccentric travelers motivated by the spirit of adventure, managed to get to know first hand, in Ethiopia, that ideal beatitude of Third World ideology: a country uncontaminated by the West.

One of those travelers, the Scotsman Bruce, arrived at Gondar (Addis Ababa still did not exist) in 1770, and found a society totally deserving of the lapidary Hobbsian characterization of the primitive state of the human horde. Life in Ethiopia, before that nation would lose the supposed beatitude of autarchy and of noncontamination by the West, was truly nasty, brutish and short. Not even the all powerful implacable vizir, Ras Miguel, had a moment free from fear. "I find myself," he confided to Bruce, "forced to fight for my life everyday." When Bruce knew Ras Miguel and the young king under his tutelage, both were busy personally gouging out the eyes from a group of prisoners. Each day in Ethiopia involved a succession of similar horrors: torture, including multilations of the hands, feet, sex organs, and death administered with maximum cruelty were banal events. The overwhelming fact of life was universal insecurity. In Bruce's account, Ras Miguel ended in the loss of his daily fight for life: his body and those of his friends were thrown to the hyenas.

The only respite in the war of all against all was brought on by bad weather. On dark and rainy days, when one was prevented from going out to the field to kill and mutilate, the court of the king of Ethiopia passed the time eating, drinking and fornicating communally. The main dish was a live cow, tightly tied, from which everyone cut off pieces with sharp knives. "The animal," writes Bruce, "bellows prodigiously."

From Ethiopia to England

Even before examples such as Ethiopia, it is not likely that Third World ideologists will retreat even an inch from the position that modernization (euphemism for Westernization) of the Third World is not a benefit, but rather the greatest evil that could have been inflicted on the African, Asiatic or Western marginal countries. Theirs is not a reasonable argument, but rather a belief anchored in emotions, or a propagandistic stand.

If we omit one or another of these two motivations or their combination (which is the most frequent case), it will be difficult for an African, Asiatic or Latin American observer (in contrast with a Western Third World ideologist, self-conditioned to see only perversity in his own society and to regard its virtues as negligible) not to discern in advanced capitalist societies certain characteristic qualities worthy of emulation.

At least in their stage of great vigor and growth, today perhaps closed in some of them, those societies have shown a uniform capacity for social discipline that is not to be explained even principally by compulsion, but rather by the presence and action of worthy ruling classes, capable of stimulating emulation and, equally or more importantly, of populations inclined to respond to this stimulus.

Since Max Weber's *The Protestant Ethic and the Spirit of Capitalism,* it has been commonplace to observe that the so-called spirit of capitalism is historically related to the Protestant reformation. The countries that broke from Rome were the same that began the initial capitalist take-off and swiftly and successfully explored the unknown land of economic freedom; of social esteem instead of reproof for merchants and ambitious artisans; of rationalism, experimental science, and technological innovation.

The correlation is not a superficial one of cause and effect. The

Protestant Reformation was only one aspect of a complex development which had at its core a new concept of man—his life on earth and, inevitably, a new concept of the relation of man to God. It was the first historically significant nationalist movement, the first generalized demand for self-determination, for countries but also for the human individual. If we see things in this way, we will understand that nationalism and capitalism were not consequences of the Protestant Reformation but that all were parts of an inextricable totality.

In the same way, the countries that permitted their kings to remain faithful to Rome and that were immediately after protagonists of the reactionary movement that was the Counter-Reformation, not only saw their economic and social development retarded, but were laggard already, before the Protestant schism, compared to others (later Protestant) that since the end of the Middle Ages had been incubating the philosophic, political, social and economic revolution that would lead them to develop what should be called not simply capitalism, but capitalist civilization.

The capitalist revolution first blossomed in England, that "nation of shopkeepers" according to a famous contemptuous expression of the anticapitalist spirit that in one way or another all reactionaries share— not just those nostalgic for feudalism and aristocracy, but socialists of all stripes. These latter consider themselves to be progressive, when their unconscious yearnings go much further back than feudalism, all the way back to tribal society.[14]

If an imaginary neutral observer, or at least one not excessively intoxicated by the Third World ideology gazes upon the original capitalist nation, today eroded by its past success (and exertions) and by socialism, he or she would find a society not without faults— because perfection exists only in the theoretical design of demonstratedly dangerous utopias—but admirable beyond question and worthy of serving as an example and stimulus to any other nation. British Third World ideologists take lightly, but any one else will be deeply impressed by how in Great Britain a genuinely democratic, and moreover stable political system regularly and peacefully generates alternative governments under which a remarkably uncorrupt civil service conducts with reasonable efficiency the diverse administrative tasks that a population has a right to expect of the state.

Our observer will see a normally disarmed police force that invests the greater part of its time and effort in preventing and repressing what, by overwhelming majority opinion and according to the letter and the spirit of the law, are crimes; a minimum part of that time and effort in the civilized and benevolent surveillance of even the most radical dissidents, short of terrorism; and almost no time or effort in committing abuses comparable to those that in too many other societies (and notably in the countries of the Third World) seem to be the principal reason for the existence of police forces.

The observer will see an army that in modern times (in coincidence with capitalist development in Great Britain) even after returning victorious from two wars, in every circumstance has been impeccably respectful and obedient of the duly elected and constituted civil authorities. He or she will see an independent uncorrupt judiciary, committed to interpreting and justly applying the laws that a free parliament has sanctioned. The observer will see not an equalitarian society, which fortunately Great Britain is not in spite of the strenuous efforts of British socialists, but one with reasonable vertical social mobility, less than in other countries which enjoy capitalist civilization but with a clear tendency to increase (in contrast with the inverse tendency toward stratification, observable in socialist societies after a few years of socialism having been established). It is a society in which the different social classes, without loving each other (which would be a high expectation) nevertheless share the clear and justified conviction of belonging to the same social and political body and of having more common interests than radical divergences. Marginality and unemployment exist, but, even with the present crisis, not in a way comparable to that justly criticized by the socialists of the nineteenth century, and moreover felt to be scandalous exactly in the same measure in which a previously achieved high level of material comfort and social security make any step backward seem unbearable.

Our imaginary neutral observer of Great Britain will also see not just the monuments, but still the live and vital expressions of an almost unbelievable national energy: the remains of empire without a doubt, but also those of an unparalleled political creativity; those of a formidable economic, technical, intellectual, and military effort; those of great literature written in a language spoken in the fifteenth century by a handful of islanders which is today, because of their effort and genius and that of their offspring, the *Lingua Franca* of the whole world.

Lastly and above all our observer will find a society that deserves to be described as humane, in which social and interpersonal relations are normally nonviolent; where courteous discussion and reasonable agreement or disagreement are preferred to confrontation; where a raised voice is so rare as to be shocking; where the newspaper vendor can leave his merchandise unguarded, quite certain that no one will take a newspaper without paying; where mistreatment of the weak and of animals is less frequent than anywhere else. It is, in short, a society free and civilized.

Before Capitalism

British society was not always like this; on the contrary, before the full development in England of capitalist civilization, with all its good and bad effects on English society, it was almost as barbaric as the Ethiopia that Bruce knew. Precapitalist England was (as precapitalist societies in general) a brutal and implacable country. The number of capital executions during the reign of Henry VIII is estimated in the tens of thousands, and this in a country with a population of less than five million. These were, moreover, public executions carried out with maximum cruelty. In 1531 Parliament approved boiling some criminals alive. In the seventeenth and eighteenth centuries public executions were still a popular and amusing entertainment.[15] In Tyburn the executioner had so much work that he literally hanged the condemned by cartloads: he fixed the noose around their necks and then moved the cart to leave them hanging. Relatives of the hanged grasped their legs with all their weight to shorten agony. In 1642 the Long Parliament closed the so-called Bear Garden, but until that time in London, and for a much longer time in other parts of England, one of the most popular spectacles was to see a chained bear, with its teeth previously broken and filed, torn to death by mastiffs. Dog fights to the death and cock fights were legal for a much longer time. A variation of the latter was the game of throwing at cocks, which consisted of half burying a cock, leaving the neck and head uncovered, and stoning it to death. A favorite pastime of Londoners during these centuries was to go to Bedlam and see the insane nude and in chains. Mothers took their young children to this spectacle.

Still during the reign of George III (concluded in 1820) there were no fewer than 160 capital crimes, with age a meaningless factor in the prosecution of a criminal: in 1735, 9-year-old Mary Wooton was condemned to death and executed in Middlesex for allegedly robbing the woman who employed her as a servant. For the sole jurisdiction of London during the twelve years of Queen Ann's reign (1701-1713) there is a registry of 242 public executions. Their popularity as entertainment had remained undiminished, and lasted until the beginning of the reign of Victoria. Until the end of the eighteenth century or the beginning of the nineteenth, hanging had not completely substituted crueler forms of capital executions. Thomas Hardy heard directly from his grandmother how a woman was burned alive in Dorchester around 1800. And executions were not the only public punishment. Much more frequent were whippings and the block; victims of the latter were stoned and covered with filth by passers by, suffering injuries sometimes resulting in death. The last public whipping registered in Saint Albans took place in 1838. The last display in the block in London was in 1830. There is record of this punishment still in 1854 in Truro.

From the brutality and insensitivity that were so notoriously characteristic of English society a short time ago, there remains practically no significant trace. How can this be explained? The answer, I dare argue, is evident. Let us imagine two curves. One represents the evolution of the level of public and private cruelty in England (and somewhat weaker but perceptible reflections in the English domains, beginning in Wales, Scotland, and Ireland, and reaching overseas colonies); the other represents the development by and in that society of capitalist civilization and sensitivity. We will see that there is correspondence between the decline of the first curve and the rise of the other. Capitalism not only has caused a prodigious economic revolution, but moreover another equally important one in sensitivity. Of this second revolution, one of the most significant products has been socialism. This Marx knew perfectly and says abundantly, in spite of his emotional prejudice against capitalist civilization. What Marx couldn't see, blinded by that prejudice, and what present day socialists persist in not admitting in spite of overwhelming proof, is that the libertarian and humanitarian ideals of socialism not only are creations of capitalist civilization, but utopian projections, besides, of virtues and practices undoubtedly imperfect, but indissolubly linked to the capitalist organization of society and incompatible with socialism.

Notes

1. Under the tyranny of Gaspar Rodriguez Francia, it was strictly prohibited to leave or enter Paraguay. The French naturalist, Aimé Bonpland, fellow traveller of Humboldt in the scientific exploration of the New World, had the bad luck of crossing the Paraguayan frontier and was detained for ten years. Bolivar interceded on behalf of Bonpland, and even threatened (in letters that received no reply) Rodriguez Francia—a sort of Paraguayan Khomeini—with a military expedition to rescue Bonpland.
2. Darcy Ribeiro, *Las Américas y la Civilización,* 3 vols. (Buenos Aires: Centro Editor de América Latina S. A., 1969), vol. 3, pp. 98-100. The words and phrases placed in quotations that follow are from the same source, in the same pages or in the immediately previous or following ones.
3. One wonders how Ribeiro would explain the exactly reverse case of

Japan, which had to give up its isolation to overcome its backwardness and prosper in the modern world.

4. Ribeiro, *Las Américas,* pp. 99-100.

5. Ibid., p. 100. "Our days" is clearly a reference to the Cuban revolution, of which Rodriguez Francia and the Lopezes would be, according to this interpretation of history, forerunners.

6. E. Bradford Burns, *The Poverty of Progress: Latin America in the Nineteenth Century* (Berkeley: University of California Press, 1980).

7. Manuel Belzu, President of Bolivia, quoted by Burns, *The Poverty of Progress,* p. 108.

8. "Playa del Tirano" is the name, to the present day, given to the spot on the Island of Margarita where Aguirre disembarked.

9. Miguel Otero Silva, Seix Barral, Barcelona, 1979.

10. There is a recent reissuance by Editorial Ateneo de Caracas, 1980.

11. That is, he was uncontaminated by Europeanization, certainly much more than Belzu, who evidently had heard of Proudhon.

12. The same according to whom Rosas, Francia, Belzu, etc. were deplorable tyrants, products of Latin American backwardness and contributors to its persistence. An example of this point of view (that Burns, Ribeiro and Fernando González would coincide in detesting as "Westernizing") is the following analysis of the reincarnation of Rosas in Perón, "Third World ideologue," by an Argentinian writer: "Rosas's tyranny was one of the saddest and most humiliating periods of our history. After twenty years of cruel despotism, during which all life and property were at the mercy of the tyrant and his minions, the Argentine people were allowed to breathe again. Once again, they dared talk freely, schools reopened, books and newspapers started appearing again, civic institutions multiplied; the citizenry, which had seen its rights drowned in blood in two decades of arbitrary rule, found its rights and dignities restored; above all, doors were opened to the outside world, allowing the Argentine people to communicate once again with the civilized countries. . . . But the irrational never wholly dies in man. The mass's 'other self,' which at any moment can transform Beethoven's fatherland into Hitler's Reich, is always [in Argentina] struggling to raise its head. This other self is angered by progress and humiliated by civilization. . . . It has never ceased its struggle to reconquer its lost primacy and to take its revenge. Disguised as the peaceful lover of local folklore, it struggles for recognition by simulating love of tradition. Many have given their support to this cause, which they thought good and useful, little knowing that they were helping bring back the dark age of history. Perónism was born with the help of reason and appeared as a remedy to manifest errors and injustices. But it was soon devoured by the negative aspects of irrationalism. Perón was attracted by the irrational, and tried to renege the [civilizing] Argentine project in favor of a plan conceived along entirely opposite lines. No question of Europe, of course: Why Europe? We are Americans, and somehow 'Indians.' Let us revert as far as possible to the cultures as they existed before the arrival and triumph of the Spanish, Greco-Roman, European culture. Let us reject as an evil shadow the memory of those who made possible the Argentina of the railways, ports, roads, and factories; who made the country one of the granaries of the world and one of its principal cattle breeders; who

transformed Argentina into a kind of El Dorado and a haven for all the needy and persecuted of Europe. All this was the work of Rivadavia, of Sarmiento, of Mitre, of Alberdi, of other great men hated today while Rosas, Facundo Quiroga and their like are praised to the skies. . . . Thus we have seen a Perónist provincial governor proclaiming: 'In this province, the names of traitors such as Rivadavia, Sarmiento, Mitre, must not be heard again.' " (Francisco Luis Bernárdez, "Nuestra Argentina," *El Nacional,* Caracas [March 14, 1975]).

13. This is true except for Christianity, which spread from Egypt to Ethiopia in the fifth century of our era and which, although surely superior in every way to the superstitions it displaced, did not manage by itself, in the absence of all economic development, to soften Ethiopian mores.

14. Karl R. Popper makes this point in *The Open Society and its Enemies,* 4th ed. (Princeton: Princeton University Press, 1963).

15. This information is found in any social history of England. For example, see R. J. Mitchell and M. D. R. Leys, *A History of the English People* (London: Longmans, Green, 1950).

6

The True Nature of Capitalism

In an excess of enthusiasm for something that is after all but a less imperfect form of social, economic, and political order than all others, some defenders of capitalist civilization at times imprudently exaggerate the advantages to be expected of the ruling of human affairs by the laws of market in the economic realm; and in the political realm, of that "free market" of ideas called pluralism. Such exaggerated enthusiasm about capitalist civilization is alien to the healthy skepticism and wise modesty of true liberalism. Genuine liberals, from Locke to Hayek, have never argued that political liberties (and their economic corollaries) are a guarantee of universal happiness and prosperity, or constitute a sufficient basis for the moral equilibrium and spiritual fulfillment of society and of individuals. Liberal wisdom denies the existence of definitive solutions, or of recipies that, administered to the social body, will resolve all antagonism and all problems as if by magic. Liberal thought[1] is founded on wariness about the illusion that human beings are, by nature, only kind and sensible, and in the observation that unrestricted power turns even the most well-intentioned into monsters. Hence the liberal rejects systems of government that either stimulate populist demagoguery or grant a man or an oligarchy (for example, a single party) powers of coercion greater than the indispensible minimum. In contrast to religions and utopias, liberalism does not promise salvation or offer the realization of absolute good in this world. It does not believe in a historical mutation by means of which all conflicts of groups and individuals among themselves and with the state can cease once and for all, but rather in the possibility of a constant examination and permanent arbitration of those conflicts, in the light of experience and reason, respecting tradition and custom, and under the rule of laws as simple as possible. Those laws must be of feasible fulfillment, so that they can normally be obeyed with a minimum of coercion. They must estipulate the separation of the public powers and generally propiciate the alternability and the broad distribution of power. And they must establish basic rights and inviolable guarantees, that minimize the probability of abuse of power by the state or by private powers against citizens.

This latter aspect of liberalism has been perverted by means of the progressive extension of the definition of the rights of man to fields that objectively demand not the inhibition of the state but its intervention. It has been supposed, with the self-sufficency of superficiality, that the great liberal theoriticians remained unaware that the power of the state can be useful and even indispensible to achieve certain ends that appear desirable. Of course they noticed this, and whoever takes time to read, for example, Adam Smith, will find in *The Wealth of Nations* precise recommendations on areas of human action that the state should not leave under the sole guidance of the "invisible hand" of the equilibrium between supply and demand. But they also noticed, and this is what socialists do not understand, that the power of state intervention, once unleashed, achieves both the desirable and the obnoxious and, by irresistible tendency, progressively more the latter. It scores successes, but becomes the source of evermore frequent and more serious abuses and mistakes.

Capitalism and Liberalism

Before liberalism became political and economic theory with Milton, Locke, and Montesquieu, and Adam Smith, it was practical human action. For the economic, political, social, and cultural results of that human action, such as they were perceived during the middle of the last century, the derogatory label of *capitalism* was coined. As that label is unerasable, it is better to accept it, while attempting to substitute for it the label *capitalist civilization* which conveys that the flowering of capitalist economies and that of liberal political systems was a single process. It was in Western Europe and more precisely in northern Italy, England and Flanders, where at the waning of the Middle Ages, bankers, merchants and manufacturers began to buy from needy feudal princes charters that permitted them to develop their mercentile activities with some security. The security thus purchased gradually extended to all towndwellers, the bourgeois, and is at the root of modern political freedoms. This has been said a thousand times before. The only reason for repeating it is to counteract the systematic effort to ignore it or cloud it on the part of the socialist polemic against capitalism. Therefore it is necessary to reiterate that the struggle of those conducting business to achieve guarantees for their activity is a key factor in the origin of democracy.

Under feudalism, private property theoretically did not exist except for the holding, by feudal lords, of land property of the crown. It took a long and hard struggle to establish the concept and the legitimacy of "bourgeois" private property and secure its protection from sudden or gradual confiscation by whimsical taxation.

The successful bourgeois effort to take this power from kings and transfer it to parliaments representative of property owners (before being representative of the whole population) unchained a mechanism of immense political importance. What began as the protection of commerce and private property—a set of privileges—became over time the rights of all in the form of guarantees and liberties of general scope.

Capitalism has been, thus, not an arbitrary construction set up to correspond to preconceived theories (as socialism is), but a natural economic and social development which led to astounding economic growth first in certain areas of western Europe, but later in the whole world, including even areas where the market economy has been either hindered by precapitalist economic primitivism or deliberately destroyed in the name of socialism (or by both factors together).

Backward or socialist (or backward *and* socialist) countries derive enormous benefit, even without wanting to and often without even realizing it, from the existence of a world capitalist market, by whose creativity they are nourished, and whose system of prices and wages serves them (in the case of the socialist economies) as the only solid reference for their otherwise wholly artificial system of central planning, which would otherwise flounder hopelessly.[2]

Capitalism is an economic system which, as experience proves, is conducive to political liberty and the growth of and respect for human rights. Under the logic of capitalism, governments cease being arbitrary and despotic, and gradually submit themselves to legal systems purposely designed for the protection of the rights of citizens and the limitation of the power of the state. This is something far more valuable than mere prosperity, and would be preferable to it if, it were possible to distinguish one thing from the other, instead of their being, as they in fact are, consubstantial.

The Beneficiaries of Capitalism

Capitalism, far from impoverishing the masses, has improved their situation beyond any sensible former expectation. Moreover, it has improved the situation of the poor much more than that of the rich. In the precapitalist societies, the rich accumulated their wealth exclusively by exploitation of the majority of the population through sundry forms of extortion, the use of religion as a tool of social iniquity and (under the guise of judicial procedures) the cruelest repression. From a gross economic product insufficient even if it had been well distributed, the lords of society (warriors or high priests) confiscated the greater part without themselves making any direct contribution to production.

Thus they enjoyed luxuries so extravagant that few of the rich today could pay for their equivalent, plus other privileges that today cannot be purchased at any price (for example, exclusive access to areas and amenities such as forests and parks that are today freely accessible to everyone). Additionally, many goods and services that were formerly great luxuries are today within reach of practically everyone in advanced capitalist countries.

The prosperity characteristic of capitalism has produced a situation where for the first time in history, masses of people compete for the enjoyment of things other than bread and shelter.

José Ortega y Gasset complains, in his essay "The Rebellion of the Masses" (1930), of the phenomenon of the "full house."[3] Through this he gave literary form to the lament of the privileged at the newfangled and shocking access of common people to services (trains, theaters, bathing resorts) that had originally been invented and developed for the rich, but, that by the unstoppable process of democratization characteristic of capitalism, were made (even in backward Spain of 1930) accessible to a large lower middle class and some workers. This is a source of anticapitalist feeling that psychoanalysis would discover in many socialists. For them, capitalism has vulgarized society; it has destroyed or is destroying and will end by erasing from the surface of the earth all that is exclusive, rare and refined.

Contrary to the socialist myth, capitalism has produced much better distribution of wealth and has modified against the rich and in favor of the majority the access to goods and services. The very rich can still buy exclusive haute couture dresses, extravagant jewels, hand tooled automobiles or private airplanes (although they no longer have highways or even air space to themselves); they can privately screen films in their own homes. But the practice of occupying public sites as if they were also their property (the "Promenade des Anglais" in Nice is today an area where no one hesitates to walk) has been taken away from them, and also exclusive access to decent shoes and clothing.

Schumpeter points out in *Capitalism, Socialism and Democracy* that the typical benefits of capitalist mass production are clothing made cheaply and of good quality, footwear accessible to everyone and transportation within the reach of all.[4] That is, things that yesterday only the rich could pay for or that, because they were nonexistent, they could not miss, and which now, because they are of general use and cause overcrowding (the full house effect that so moritified Ortega) have spoiled their exclusive pleasure. The trend started, of course, with the industrial revolution. In a sense identical to Ortega's complaint, Talleyrand lamented (or boasted) that those who had not known the ancient regime did not know how sweet life could be. Schumpeter clarifies Talleyrand's remarks: "electric lighting, universal and cheap wherever capitalist civilization has reached, is only a marginal improvement for those rich enough to buy any number of candles and pay servants to take care of them." He says further: "Queen Elizabeth had silk stockings. What is typical of Capitalism is not producing more silk stockings for Queens, but in putting them within the reach of the factory workers as reward for a continually decreasing work effort."[5] The economic results of capitalism are "an avalanche of consumer goods that deepens and widens the reach of real income, and that consists of articles for mass consumption, so that the purchasing power of the wage dollar increases more than that of any other dollar. The capitalist process progressively increases the standards of living of the masses, and not by accident, but rather by virtue of its own mechanism."[6]

Capitalism has also shown a secular tendency toward the equalization of incomes that persists in being ignored or underestimated in spite of crushing evidence. For instance *Le Jardin du Voisin* by Jean Fourastié and Béatrice Bazil (1980), shows how in the first years of the nineteenth century the families of top government officials in France (which means not the richest Frenchmen, but those whose incomes can be found in records) had incomes 82 times higher than the workers with the lowest salaries. In 1900 the ratio was still 20 to 1; but it had become 10 to 1 in 1939, and today is less than 7 to 1. This gigantic revolution would still be relatively little understood without the observation that in 1800, three-fourths of the French population was at the lowest income levels, as opposed to 10 percent today. And a similar evolution, with variations, has taken place in all capitalist countries, with New Zealand, a "dependent" country and an exporter of raw materials and food,[7] at the head of the capitalist egalitarianism.

The history of France or of any other capitalist country, especially those with high levels of industrialization, records that the take-off toward capitalist civilization caused serious social upheavals in each case proportional to the rapid increase of productivity and production. This is at the base of some of the most classical objections to capitalism, which consist of reasoning (or feeling) that the price exacted by the new system is excessive, and that the capitalist system in its beginnings (a moment that to these observers appeared as defining a permanent condition) was harsher on the mass of humanity than any previous one.

Those who reasoned or felt so could not perceive that capitalism is not comparable to any previous system, for the simple reason that no system before capitalism had even imagined the possibility of producing wealth on such a scale and opening for the first time the possibility of rescuing the human masses from hopeless deprivation. Furthermore, if we take into account the dismal situation of mankind everywhere before the capitalist revolution, the social upheavals of early capitalist development hardly seem a high price to pay for the benefits society obtains in return, which include the political liberties inherent in a market economy. It is true that those benefits have been discernible in their entirety only later, and they have recently been further enhanced by comparison with the visible failure and the much greater suffering caused by socialism after 1917. But Marx and Engels in the *Communist Manifesto* bear witness that the gigantic advance of mankind caused by the capitalist revolution was clearly discernible to penetrating minds even at the moment of greatest capitalist perturbation of the stagnant water of late feudal society. It was also Marx and Engels who first saw through the reactionary roots of some socialists' rejections of the capitalist revolution.[8]

As for the possibility, now that capitalism has opened the way, of achieving equal or better economic and political results (prosperity plus freedom) through socialism, that is, by abolishing private property and free economic initiative, the least that can be said is that it has not happened anywhere. The outcome is that inferior economic and political results have been obtained in the socialist countries—and first in the Soviet Union—at a very high price in human suffering, which has been more extensive, enduring and severe than than the worst suffering caused by early capitalism.

Capitalist Civilization

Capitalism is not only an economic system. Its fabric is woven with all other aspects of human action, ambition, imagination and sensitivity that were present at its genesis, that developed together with it, and that in many cases flourished because of it. One would blush to repeat something so trite and so Marxist if it were not constantly denied by an unscrupulous and superficial propaganda, according to which all that is estimable in modern civilization has developed without connection and even against the grain of the economic system that has been at the root of that civilization.

A fashionable anthropological and historiographical proposition extravagantly praises primitive or traditional cultures, not with a scientific spirit, but out of anticapitalist prejudice and the determination to find in or attribute to those primitive or traditional cultures values supposedly superior because uncontaminated by civilization—the primitive cultures—or by capitalist utilitarianism and individualism—the precapitalist, traditional cultures.

There are here two points of view. One admires industrial civilization just as Marx admired and hailed it, but sees in it (unlike Marx) an achievement of men in spite of the economic system that has been at its base. The second point of view, more logically, professes a hatred of both capitalism and the civilization that capitalism has created. With relation to this second point of view, there is not much one can say. It is pointless to argue with people who believe that mankind was happy, unalienated, and securely and serenely placed in the world when it was just another animal species, like lizards and monkeys. It must be said, contrarily, that the realities of even the most primitive societies, the most "uncontaminated" by civilization, do not correspond to the unpolluted mythical moment when man supposedly was not yet the flaw in the diamond of the world. The myth of the innocence and happiness of man before the fall and that of the noble savage are not identical. The noble savage already has individuality, already is a man and not an animal among the animals, has already fallen. Any form of communism that biased anthropologists may have been able to attribute to some primitive society, would be due less to primitive innocence than to utter privation of material goods and of any other element capable of favoring the emergence of the individual and the beginning of the "antinatural" processes of high human cultures and civilization.

The first point of view, which combines admiration for industrial society with the strange idea that it has developed in spite of capitalism, is unfounded. Long before the modern rise of the productive forces that have permitted for the first time to glimpse the end of all poverty, former fundamental forward steps (such as the substitution of magical thought by rational thought) have their remote origin in the same virtues (or faults) of the human species that have come to full flowering in the capitalist revolution and its civilization.

According to Schumpeter,[9] rational thought and behavior originated in a slow but incessant expansion of the context within which individuals or human groups, upon confronting concrete situations (and to get out of them with minimum damage or with the greatest benefit possible) discovered that it was preferable to act in accordance with those rules of coherence that much later were called logic. This rational attitude first penetrated the human spirit because of economic necessity.

> The rational attitude presumably forced itself on the human mind primarily from economic necessity; it is the everyday economic task to which we as a race owe our elementary training in rational thought and behavior—I have no hesitation in saying that all logic is derived from the pattern of the economic decision or, to use a pet phrase of mine, that the economic pattern is the matrix of logic.[11]

The process of the rationalization of primitive thought by the pressure of life or death choices cannot be connected to a capitalist civilization that would not emerge until many millenia later; but, on the other hand, it is doubtless that capitalism

> exalts the monetary unit—not itself a creation of capitalism—into a unit of account. That is to say, capitalist practice turns the unit of money into a tool of rational cost-profit calculations, of which the towering monument is double-entry bookkeeping. Without going into this, we will notice that, primarily a product of the evolution of economic rationality, the cost-profit calculus in turn reacts upon that rationality; by crystallizing and defining it numerically, it powerfully propels the logic of enterprise. And thus defined and quantified for the economic sector, this type of logic or attitude or method then starts upon its conqueror's career subjugating—rationalizing—man's tools and philosophies, his medical practice, his picture of the cosmos, his outlook on life, everything in fact including his concepts of beauty and justice and his spiritual ambitions.

> In this respect it is highly significant that modern mathematico-experimental science developed, in the fifteenth, sixteenth and seventeenth centuries, not only along with the social process usually referred to as the Rise of Capitalism, but also outside the fortress of scholastic thought and in the face of its contemptuous hostility. In the fifteenth century mathematics was mainly concerned with questions of commercial arithmetic and the problems of the architect. The utilitarian mechanical device, invented by men of the craftsman type, stood at the source of modern

physics. The rugged individualism of Galileo was the individualism of the rising capitalist class. The surgeon began to rise above the midwife and the barber. The artist who at the same time was an engineer and an entrepreneur—the type immortalized by such men as Vinci, Alberti, Cellini; even Dürer busied himself with plans for fortifications—illustrates best of all what I mean. By cursing it all, scholastic professors in the Italian universities showed more sense than we give them credit for. The trouble was not with individual unorthodox propositions. Any decent schoolman could be trusted to twist his texts so as to fit the Copernican system. But those professors quite rightly sensed the spirit behind such exploits—the spirit of rationalist individualism, the spirit generated by rising capitalism.[12]

It is interesting to compare Schumpeter's penetrating analysis with the following passage from Frantz Fanon: "Against the unconditional affirmation of European culture, there has risen, (among African intellectuals) the unconditional affirmation of African culture . . . the bards of negritude now oppose young-Africa to ancient Europe, poetry to boring reason, energetic nature to oppressive logic; on one side, naiveté, petulance, liberty and, why not, lust, and also irresponsibility; on the other, rigidity, ceremony, protocol, skepticism."[13]

An economic (and therefore social) evolution that began with barter and slavery that has culminated, in capitalism, with industrialism, modern finance and politcial liberties could be admitted to represent the "fall" with relation to a mythical innocence and primitive irresponsibility. But it has also been (even if we were to believe in primitive innocence and in the virtues and happiness of savages) the ladder upon which mankind has reached an astonishing productivity and achieved the height of rational thought, established the experimental scientific method, and cultivated respect for the dignity and the rights of man.

Socialism has managed to propagate a diffuse animosity against capitalism, seeing it as an infection in the social body. This animosity has managed to blur the indivisible line of capitalism with institutions and achievements that are not only not perceived as an integral part of capitalist civilization, but that are taken as examples of direct victories against capitalism, or in any case, as areas of progress created by anticapitalists against the grain of a nefarious system that measures everything in terms of costs and benefits.

Let us take, proposes Schumpeter, the case of nonprofit public hospitals. These are taken to be a concession torn from hated capitalism, when in reality, they are a

product of capitalism not only, to repeat, because the capitalist
process supplies the means and the will, but much more fundamentally because capitalist rationality supplied the habits of
mind that evolved the methods used in these hospitals. And the
victories, not yet completely won but in the offing, over cancer,
syphilis and tuberculosis will be as much capitalist achievements
as motorcars or pipe lines or Bessemer steel have been. In the
case of medicine, there is a capitalist profession behind the
methods, capitalist both because to a large extent it works in a
business spirit and because it is an emulsion of the industrial and
commercial bourgeoisie. But even if that were not so, modern
medicine and hygiene would still be by-products of the capitalist
process just as is modern education.[14]

And there is more. The habit of calculating costs and benefits
induces a utilitarian but also an anti-Machiavellian ethic, expressed in
the well-known maxim according to which honesty is the best policy.
In our century the leaders—Wilson and Roosevelt—of the capitalist
country par excellence, have been the ones who during two world wars
and at their conclusion formulated non-Machiavellian, idealistic proposals about the way to conduct international relations.

Characteristically, the highest goal of this new organization of world
affairs should be peace. All rationalism is pacifist and antiheroic, and
capitalism is so to the utmost degree. Warfare disturbs economic
activity. Those who despise "merchants" as unwarlike (which they
are) and therefore inferior, have been throughout history the initiators
of wars. Businessmen fear war, because it is a noncalculable risk, and
because in times of war, the heroic reckless values (and the human
types) of pre-capitalist society prevail. Socialists have used and abused
their reference to the armament merchants (a sector of the capitalist
economy much less important to it than its equivalent in the socialist
economies), but they cannot hide the fact that the shares traded in the
important world stock markets of the capitalist world invariably fall in
price (and the price of the "barbarian relic" that is gold rises) at the
outbreak of any crisis capable of leading to war; and on the other hand
rise to greet any event whose net effect is to diminish international
tensions.

To summarize, capitalism has not been the enemy of culture and
peace. Capitalist civilization is consubstantial with the most formidable and unforeseen rise of specifically human values. Unfortunately,
wars have not therefore ended, but rather are waged much more
destructively with those creations of capitalist civilization that are

experimental science and industrialism. But this is not because of capitalism, it is in spite of it. Aggressiveness and corresponding defense reflexes are rooted in the individual and in society at a level that is not even precapitalist, but literally prehuman.

The Fox and the Grapes

When Engels was still alive (he died in 1895), those who dreamed of burying capitalism according to Marxist precepts began to seriously worry over the growing evidence that the capitalist system, far from pauperizing the masses, was rapidly rescuing them from deep poverty for the first time in history. From then on socialists have introduced several additional objections to capitalism, some inspired by the global and structural criticism that Marx made, and some divergent, novel, and even contradictory of Marxist orthodoxy. Some of these objections persist in being of an economic nature, although without the totalizing power of unadulterated Marxism. They point to the survival within the capitalist economy, in spite of astonishing progress, of inequalities and of cycles of prosperity and depression.

But those economic arguments, although worthy of attention in that they show true problems that require attention, have lost force as the basis of a revolutionary praxis, especially when we know the utter economic failure of "real socialism." Capitalism each day gives additional proof of clear and overwhelming superiority over socialism in the areas of production and income distribution, and even social security.

Therefore we have seen totally novel anticapitalist arguments rise and assume first order of importance, or a new emphasis on ones that previously were only complementary to the central socialist thesis. According to this thesis socialism could easily produce sufficient wealth to distribute it to each according to his needs and lift mankind from the realm of need, characteristic of all previous history, to the realm of freedom, supposedly to be inaugurated by the socialists simply by confiscating the means of production (such as they were in, for example, England in 1890) and thus liberating them of the shackles and perverse and artificial inhibitions implicit in an "historically obsolete mode of production."[15]

The fallacy and abysmal naiveté of that expectation having been shown in practice, a whole new family of anticapitalist arguments is now based not on the premise that socialism could easily produce an abundance of goods greater than capitalism, and even limitless and unimaginable, but to the contrary, paradoxically, on the evils of the discredited "consumer society." This new hydra, far from being a benefit to mankind through the satisfactions it offers and the fact that it is within reach of more people, including masses of workers, is held to cause a materialistic and vulgar corruption of society.

The aspiration of human beings (the anticapitalists now tell us) should not be selfish comfort, decent clothing and shoes, household appliances, a varied diet, a roof over one's head, a car, paid vacations. Men ought to strive, rather, toward fraternal collectivist austerity and even asceticism. That, and not vulgar abundance, will be the shining path through which future generations will reach some day (perhaps within a thousand years, as Mao Tse Tung did not hesitate to say) the perfect happiness of communism. The "new man" in Cuba, Vietnam, or Cambodia does not own anything and consumes very little, but we are told that he is free. He has the joy of knowing that his sacrifice and that of his children, grandchildren, great-grandchildren, and who knows how many generations more, are well employed in the construction of socialism and in bringing closer, even if by an infinitely small fraction of time, the inevitable advent of communism[16]. What no one has explained is why a historical development proclaimed to be inevitable must demand sacrifices that go from renunciation of the consumer society, that could exist today in Czechoslovakia or East Germany, to the massacre of the majority of a nation, as in Cambodia.

Anticapitalist Ecologism

A novel complement to the exhortation not to touch or taste the cursed fruits of the consumer society (since socialism will not yield them) is a strident alarmism about the ecological balance of the planet. It is far from my intention to suggest that there is not a serious and real problem in environmental pollution. At the same time it seems evident that the motivation of at least some of the prophets of this new apocalypse is not entirely humanistic or scientific, but rather inspired by the hatred of capitalist civilization. Because capitalism, where it has functioned reasonably well, has generated abundance and liberty, it will be necessary to preach that that very fact proves its evil nature. And because, evidently, socialism spontaneously and inevitably generates scarcity and rigid social control, that will be proclaimed as one of its virtues (unforeseen by Marx). Just as wars and other great catastrophes require ruthless governments, capable of suppressing consumption and extracting other great sacrifices from populations, it is said or suggested that only socialist statism can administer the increasingly scarce resources available to an increasingly large world population.[17]

One cannot lightly dismiss the possibility that the world may in the future face such emergencies and catastrophes as to require the imposition by force of authoritarian or totalitarian leadership, even where capitalism and democracy once flourished. But the socialists will on their side have to admit that such a justification for socialism is not only different, but totally opposed to the socialist promises according to which only private property stood in the way of the realm of freedom, based upon an unlimited abundance of goods, and reachable from one day to the next just by seizing the means of production from the capitalists.

Moreover, the somber perspective of a world ungovernable except by socialist despotism is not ineluctable. Today we know, thanks to capitalist civilization, that the creativity of the human species is immensely superior to anything that could have been dreamed of. Moreover there is good reason and evidence to suspect that the still unexplored resources of the human brain are so vast that they can be described as inexhaustible.

Today, socialism is no longer a utopian project, but a concrete system tested in diverse societies, each one having its unique situation. It appears obvious from these very divergent cases that captialism has not only resulted in more progress and less suffering than socialism, but also, clearly, that it increases the possibilities (as socialism does not) for the discovery of ever new creative responses to existing problems and to those, not now imaginable, that will emerge in the future.

In contrast, socialist societies have shown themselves reactionary and obtuse, discouraging and even intolerant of the infinitely rich and unexpected initiatives of which individuals and private organizations are capable. In thought, in scientific investigation, in heterodox ideas, in the development of new techniques, socialism invariably establishes a scholastic and authoritarian orthodoxy, where canonical texts interpreted arbitrarily by a conservative (when not obscurantist) gerontocracy, determine what areas will receive the preferential investment of the limited resources of society.

There is in this a multiple loss: a loss of material resources as well as a loss of the unforeseeable creativity of human beings when they act freely and in the pursuit of their personal ends (which are not only monetary profit, although this is the most powerful spring of human action). It is totally characteristic that the discovery of the problem of environmental pollution and of the danger of ecological catastrophe on a world scale has been made in the advanced capitalist societies, and that it is in them (and not in the socialist countries) where the problem is being faced and researched. It is in capitalist civilizations that there is a constant ferment of ideas and, what is more important, of challenges to the powerful, to those who because they are in position of privilege, resist change. Therefore, the solutions to the problems of industrial society will be found, if anywhere, within capitalist civilization, and not in the suffocating environment of socialist systems where the incumbent dictator is, by astonishing coincidence, the first philosopher of the country, and sometimes of the world if not of all history.

The Example of the Cities

The problems characteristic of industrial society, and the way that capitalist civilization goes about finding solutions to them, are well illustrated by the growth of cities. That growth is undoubtedly a product of capitalism but is not (as is sometimes superficially believed) only or principally due to the concentration of population that is characteristic of industrialism. Such growth is due, above all, to the surprising improvement of environmental health under capitalism. Well into the nineteenth century there had never been cities that had managed to maintain, and much less to increase their population without a constant rural influx. The deplorable sanitary conditions of urban agglomerations caused everywhere shocking death rates. The defeat, by capitalism, of endemic diseases such as tuberculosis, typhus, and gastroenteritis, together with an immensely greater agricultural productivity in capitalist countries, freeing masses from the land, has created in the last 100 years the now familiar ever-growing megalopolis. But the first factor—the defeat of disease—has been more prevalent because even in societies with very low agricultural productivity, elementary environmental health measures introduced by the West or copied from it are sufficient to produce the phenomenon of urban explosion.

But let us turn to the subject at hand, which is the exemplary way in which capitalist civilization finds solutions to the same problems it gives rise to. One hundred years ago any projection by experts (supposing that the best would have been employed, which is doubtful, and not bureaucrats) on the desirable evolution of those fine flowers of capitalism which are modern London, Paris or New York, would have concluded that all further growth would have to stop. Each problem of those burgeoning cities would have been imagined to be insoluble in the middle or even short term, if the perverse concentration of population in reduced spaces were to continue. To take a single problem: both the central congestion and the outward increase in the absolute area of those cities should in the very short run have made transportation impossible. Distances were rapidly becoming excessive and increasingly difficult to negotiate. And if there had been no other argument, what was to be done with the mountains of manure excreted by the indispensible multitude of horses? A socialist government would have solved the problem, characteristically, by forbidding all further growth of London, Paris, or New York: a halt to any further rural immigration into the cities in search of better living conditions. And if the vegetative growth of the urban population would not cease, then a socialist government would not have thought twice about throwing city dwellers back to the countryside. We have the example close at hand: it happened in Cambodia.

Bureaucratic experts or a socialist government would not have imagined (and much less would have discovered, invented or developed) the generation and multiple uses of electricity, the internal combustion engine, macadam or asphalt pavement, nor the general multitude of technological innovations contributed by the free and ingenious initiative of myriad individuals and business corporations in the capitalist economy, and that have permitted London, Paris, New York and many other cities in the last one hundred years to undergo literally unimaginable growth.

The incorrigible paternalist—or worse, authoritarian— spirit of the socialists will reply that it would have been better for people to remain in the countryside. But where the people have wanted to be, for many and very good reasons, is in the cities, and only intellectual arrogance, together with ignorance of the facts, scorn for common people and a stupid idealization of rural life based on the experience of weekends in the country, can lead to presume that one knows better than they themselves where commonfolk should reside; and that if they do not know what's best for them, it should be, even precluding persuasion, rammed down their throats.

The collapse of the megalopolis has not taken place, but it goes on being forecast for tomorrow or the day after, with arguments surely similar to that of the intolerable accumulation of horse manure. Meanwhile, Soviet socialism has not been able to avoid the excessive growth of Moscow and Leningrad, in the same degree that advances in medicine and sanitary measures imitated from the West have caused the self-multiplication of the population of those cities. Rural immigration has not been an important factor, since almost half the population of the Soviet Union continues to be more or less forcibly tied to the land. And surely the most astute of the Soviet leaders are attentive to all western innovations that contribute to the persistent viability of the capitalist megalopolis.

Socialism, in order to function even in its renowned wasteful and inefficient way, is nourished by capitalist civilization. Of the formidable Soviet apparatus dedicated to gathering information in the West, a very important part is specialized in technological espionage, which is readily understandable if we consider that not a single industrial technique worthy of being adopted in the West has originated in the so-called socialist world.

If such is the record in the area of industrial production that is ideologically neutral and in which so much human sacrifice and capital has been invested by the Soviet Union, can we be surprised if the same or more barrenness is observable in the field of ideas and artistic creation? If we take, for example, the area of the social sciences, we will find that with the exception of the contributions of Lenin, Trotsky, and some other representatives of the first revolutionary generation, the Soviet Union has not produced since 1917 a book, a pamphlet, or even an article that represents an original, meaningful or lasting contribution to sociology, psychology, anthropology, political science or history.

This applies also (perhaps above all) for original thinking on socialism. For example, in *The Great Turning Point of Socialism* by Roger Garaudy, of almost one hundred references to books, articles and other publications in its footnotes, only three refer to bibliographic sources that are specifically Soviet (of course, the texts of Lenin or Stalin are not Soviet in that sense): *The "official" History of the USSR, The "official" History of the Russian Communist Party,* and the *Statistical Yearbook of the USSR.*

Notes

1. The adjective *liberal* and the noun *liberalism* can be vague and confusing. They are clarified by F. A. Hayek in *The Constitution of Liberty* (Chicago: University of Chicago Press, 1960), pp. 295-411 ("postscript, Why I am Not a Conservative"). Hayek begins by differentiating between liberalism and conservatism.

   > [The latter] by its very nature . . . cannot offer an alternative to the direction in which we are moving. It may succeed by its resistance to current tendencies in slowing down undesirable developments, but, since it does not indicate another direction, it cannot prevent their

continuance. It has, for this reason, invariably been the fate of conservatism to be dragged along a path not of its own choosing.

One of the fundamental traits of conservative attitude is a fear of
change, a timid distrust of the new as such, while the liberal position is
based on courage and confidence, on a preparedness to let change run
its course even if we cannot predict where it will lead. There would not
be much to object to if the conservatives merely disliked too rapid
change in institutions and public policy; here the case for caution and
slow process is indeed strong. But the conservatives are inclined to use
the powers of government to prevent change or to limit its rate to
whatever appeals to the more timid mind. In looking forward, they lack
the faith in the spontaneous forces of adjustment which makes the
liberal accept changes without apprehension, even though he does not
know how the necessary adaptations will be brought about. It is,
indeed, part of the liberal attitude to assume that, especially in the
economic field, the self-regulating forces of the market will somehow
bring about the required adjustments to new conditions, although no
one can foretell how they will do this in a particular instance. The
conservative feels safe and content only if he is assured that some
higher wisdom watches and supervises change, only if he knows that
some authority is charged with keeping the change 'orderly.'

This fear of trusting uncontrolled social forces is closely related to two
other characteristics of conservatism: its fondness for authority and its
lack of understanding of economic forces. Since it distrusts both
abstract theories and general principles, it neither understands those
spontaneous forces on which a policy of freedom relies nor possesses a
basis for formulating principles of policy. Order appears to the conservatives as the result of the continuous attention of authority, which,
for the purpose, must be allowed to do what is required by the
particular circumstances and not to be tied to rigid rule.

This is difficult to reconcile with the preservation of liberty. In general,
it can probably be said that the conservative does not object to
coercion or arbitrary power so long as it is used for what he regards as
the right purposes. He believes that if government is in the hands of
decent men, it ought not be too much restricted by rigid rules. Since he
is essentially opportunist and lacks principles, his main hope must be
that the wise and the good will rule—not merely by example, as we all
must wish, but by authority given to them and enforced by them.

The liberal is very much aware that we do not know all the answers and
that he is not sure that the answers he has are certainly the right ones or
even that we can find all the answers. He also does not disdain to seek
assistance from whatever non-rational institutions or habits have
proved their worth. The liberal differs from the conservative in his
willingness to face this ignorance and to admit how little we know,
without claiming the authority of supernatural sources of knowledge
where his reason fails him. It has to be admitted that in some respects
the liberal is fundamentally a skeptic—but it seems to require a certain
degree of diffidence to let others seek their happiness in their own

fashion and to adhere consistently to that tolerance which is an essential characteristic of liberalism. (F. A. Hayek, *The Constitution of Liberty* [Chicago: University of Chicago Press, 1960], pp. 295-411.)

2. Oil is, in this context, a good touchstone: the variations of its price in the world market tend to prevail within the so-called "socialist world," and any difference that persists, for any reason, is explicitly or implicitly understood as an arbitrary deviation from the norm supplied by the capitalist world market.

3.   There is one fact which, whether for good or ill, is of utmost importance in the public life of Europe at the present moment. This fact is the accession of the masses to complete social power. . . . Perhaps the best line of approach to this historical phenomenon may be found by turning our attention to a visual experience, stressing one aspect of our epoch which is plain to our very eyes. . . . I shall call it the fact of agglomeration, of "plenitude." Towns are full of people, houses full of tenants, hotels full of guests, trains full of travellers, cafés full of customers, parks full of promenaders, consulting-rooms of famous doctors full of patients, theatres full of spectators, and beaches full of bathers. What previously was, in general, no problem, now begins to be an everyday one, namely, to find room. . . . We see the multitude, as such, in possession of the places and the instruments created by the civilization. (José Ortega y Gassett, *The Revolt of the Masses* [New York: W. W. Norton, 1957] pp. 11-12).

4. Page 102 of the Spanish edition of this work by Aguilar, Madrid-Mexico-Buenos Aires, 1961. Even Schumpeter would have been surprised to the point of incredulity if someone had told him that in 1981 oil would reach a price of more than $30 per barrel, and that nevertheless it would be possible to fly from London to New York for less than $200 (that is, for less than thirty 1940 dollars.)

5. Ibid.

6. Ibid.

7. Jean Fourastié and Béatrice Bazil, *Le Jardin du voisin* (Paris: Hachette, collection "Pluriel," 1980), pp. 148, 155, 209.

8. Numeral I of Section III of *The Communist Manifesto* precisely bears the title: "Reactionary Socialism."

9. Joseph A. Schumpeter, *Capitalism, Socialism and Democracy* (New York: Harper & Brothers, 1962), pp. 121-26.

10. Ibid., pp. 122-23.

11. Ibid., p. 126.

12. Ibid., p. 127.

13. Frantz Fanon, *The Wretched of the Earth* (New York: Grove Press, 1963).

14. Schumpeter, *Capitalism* pp. 125-26.

15. Lest it be supposed that I am exaggerating, let me quote from Lenin: "This expropriation will facilitate an enormous development of productive forces. And seeing how capitalism is already retarding this development to an incredible degree, seeing how much progress could be achieved even on the basis of the present level of modern technique, we are entitled to say with the fullest confidence that the expropriation of the capitalists will inevitably result in an enormous development of the productive forces of human society." (Lenin, *The State and Revolution*, 2 vols, in *The Essen-*

tials of Lenin, vol. 2 [London: Lawrence & Wishart, 1947], p. 206.) Administering such fantastic and easy abundance should not be difficult either, since according to Lenin "the accounting and control necessary for this have been simplified by capitalism to an extreme and reduced to the extraordinarily simple operations—which any literate person can perform—of checking and recording, knowledge of the four rules of arithmetic, and issuing receipts." (Ibid., p. 210.)

16. Thus socialism has unexpectedly reached a position that fits in remarkably well with ancient and deeply rooted ascetic and antimercantile religious beliefs—the very beliefs it had earlier rejected as obscurantist and deceitful, hatched by priests to fool men promising them "pie in the sky" to make out for the absence of bread in this world.

17. Those ecologists who claim that only socialism can save the planet from depredation against nature caused by the greed of capitalist businessmen, carefully ignore the fact that the Soviet Union is surely the greatest delinquent in the industralist aggression against the environment, and at the same time they seem not to have heard, for example, of the success of Great Britain in cleaning the air of London and the water of the Thames. In a recent paper on the surprising increase in infant mortality in the Soviet Union, we read that the atmospheric contamination of Soviet cities is worse than that of Japan; and other ecological abuses include the misuse of pesticides and fertilizers, the contamination of water by industrial effluents, and the radiation emitted by nuclear plants of primitive design, built negligently with few safety considerations. (Christopher Davies and Murray Feshbach, *Rising Infant Mortality in the USSR in the 1970s* [United States Bureau of the Census, Series P-95, No. 74, September 1980]).

7

Wealth and Poverty of Nations, I

The preceding pages offer a new perspective from which to judge the causes of the backwardness and poverty of the Third World. They also allow us to understand the principal importance assumed by the Third World ideology as an apology of socialism and a condemnation of capitalism. The successive socialist illusions with the Soviet Union, Yugoslavia, China, Cuba, and Vietnam have been shattered. There remains but one arrow in the formerly formidable socialist arsenal: the Third World ideology which asserts that capitalism owes its success, and the rest of the world its backwardness and poverty, to the imperialist relation. Only around this thesis can a last stand be made by all those who for one reason or another persist in believing in socialist historicism. Therefore it is worthwhile to insist on the true causes of the wealth and poverty of nations.

The First Industrial Revolution

Let us stop to consider the origin and development of any of the great growth sectors which successively bore the development of the modern capitalist economies (coal, the steam engine, mechanized textile industry, electricity, machine tools, the chemical industry and, more recently, the communications and electronics and information industries). We see that all of these elements, spring and backbone of the capitalist industrial societies (and copied in the socialist industrial societies), were the natural result of, and conceived, gestated and born in the societies that pioneered capitalism as a consequence of their habits, attitudes, traditions, preexisting technologies, philosophy, world view, raw materials and institutions. On the other hand, the habits, attitudes, traditions, technologies, philosophies, world view and institutions characteristic of countries of the Third World are on the whole different from those of the pioneer capitalist countries; so it is not surprising that Third World countries find it difficult to efficiently run and maintain even simple ready-made industrial plants bought from the West or Japan.

The present Third World polemic against the West claims that capital accumulation and technological advance in the pioneer capitalist countries began only with the imperial expansion and colonial exploitation in Asia, Africa, and Latin America. Blithely set aside is the fact, registered in any economic history, that from the eleventh century on, Western Europe knew an intense period of technological advance, industrial development and creation of wealth, and that the eleventh and twelfth centuries were one of the most fertile epochs in all history for innovation in technology and industrial organization.[1]

One of the characteristics of this first industrial revolution (without which the most noted second one would not have taken place) was an explosive advance in demography. More numerous populations on the move cleared vast spaces for cultivation; cities grew; new economic conditions favored the economic initiative of the already growing bourgeoisie. There appeared again a human type, the businessman, that had vanished since the collapse of Rome. Capitalist companies were founded whose shares were negotiable. A keen industrial competition developed. The new businessmen organized their workshops on the basis of the division of labor to increase productivity. There arose a proto-proletariat quite different from medieval craftsmen.

Another characteristic of this first industrial revolution in the West was the rapid increase in the practical use of energy. Technical innovations increased the output of windmills and watermills. Numerous tasks traditionally done by hand were now entrusted to specially designed machines. Agricultural productivity, a requirement of industrial take-off, also increased. Nutrition improved and diets became more varied, and the general standard of living rose.

This rapid expansion of industry created problems that are familiar to us, for example, pollution of rivers. The search for mineral raw materials intensified, and miners obtained for that reason a privileged treatment. The growth of this early European capitalism gave rise to the first improved methods of accounting, and banking came into being. We already had the opportunity in this book to see the close relation between the birth and development of capitalism and the entirely correlative rise of rationalism and the experimental scientific spirit.

That first industrial revolution of the middle ages created the technology upon which, four centuries later, the second industrial revolution would be based. The Renaissance (which was the time of the first explorations and imperialist conquest) made a relatively small additional contribution to the technology that formed the base for that industrial take-off of England in the eighteenth and nineteenth centuries. Before the Renaissance, Western Europe had developed a mechanization without precedent in any previous civilization.

Right here we have one of the determining factors of the modern advance of the West over the rest of the world. In antiquity machines were made, but were used as toys. The Middle Ages for the first time substituted machines for manual work. The Roman historian Suetonius tells of an engineer who had invented a device that would have permitted at low cost and with little human effort, hoisting enormous marble blocks to the top of the hill of the Capitol in Rome; he was rewarded by Emperor Vespasian only on condition that the device not be used, as it would have replaced the work of too many slaves. The engineers of antiquity invented the camshaft, but used it only to move automata and other toys. The Chinese independently invented it, but did not use it except in a rudimentary rice peeler. Likewise, other Chinese inventions such as the printing press, gunpowder, the compass were kept secret or restricted, so that they did not influence the economic development of the society. In Europe, on the other hand, the discovery of the camshaft in the Middle Ages was to be crucial in the later industrialization of the West.

The Meaning and Importance of the Clock

A tenacious schoolbook mythology persists in picturing the Middle Ages as static and obscurantist, a picture fitting the Third World ideology like a glove. According to the ideology, the capitalist revolution was fortuitous and caused only by the advantages of imperialism and colonial exploitation. Unfortunately for that fable and luckily for the truth, modern historiography has collected facts demonstrating that industrialism, the opening to rationalism and new ideas, and therefore the conditions of modernization and unprecedented economic growth, all have deep roots in the West. Gilbert de Tournai speaks the enlightened medieval mind when he writes: "We will never move nearer the truth if we remain content with what is written. . . . Those who wrote before us are not our lords, but rather our guides. Truth is open to all, and has not yet been possessed entirely by anyone."[2] And Bernard, teacher in the Episcopal School of Chartres between 1114 and 1119 turns a phrase (repeated almost textually by Pascal more than 600 years later) that is at once true and clever, appropriate for not offending the dogma prevalent at the time: "We are dwarfs mounted on the shoulders of giants. Thus we see more and farther than they, not because we have better sight or a greater size, but because they carry us and bear us at their gigantic height."[3]

Teachings such as these made the men of the period accept technical inventions as something normal. And in fact "the ambition of medieval inventors was limitless."[4] Of all the machines invented and perfected in the West during the Middle Ages, none was more profoundly meaningful than the clock. Already in the thirteenth century medieval engineers had perfected the weight-driven clock, destined to play a very important role in the development of the technology of the Western world. But the greatest marvel would be, in the fourteenth century, the movement of mechanical clockwork. There had earlier been a mechanical clock in China, additional demonstration that the take-off of industrialism depends on complex factors. Even great individual genius will remain sterile if at work within a culture that does not welcome mechanization and standardization. The Chinese clock was constructed in the eleventh century of our era, but the official astronomers jealously kept the secret, considered as one of the pillars of imperial authority. It behooved the exclusively privileged emperor to promulgate the calendar. Anyone outside court circles interested in constructing a device for measuring time, would have fallen under suspicion of plotting to overthrow the dynasty. The result was that by convulsions and dynastic changes the Chinese mechanical clock ceased to function and finally disappeared before the fifteenth century. Until recently, the West had no evidence that it had existed.

A few years before the final disappearance of the Chinese mechanical clock, the Italian Giovanni Dondi, of Padua, made a surprisingly similar machine, but far from hiding it or giving it to some prince for his secret enjoyment, Dondi wrote a treatise of more than 130,000 words to explain how he had constructed it, how to arrange and decipher the quadrants, how to fix the time, how to repair it. That description is so perfect that on the basis of it, the masterwork of Dondi has been duplicated. There is a facsimile in the Smithsonian Institution in Washington, and another in the Museum of Science in London. But, much more decisively, in its own time the work of Dondi could be admired and copied by astronomers, engineers, and others interested. For a long time it served as a prototype for the construction of numerous other astronomical clocks in the great cities of Western Europe. From the second half of the fourteenth century, such clocks became common. Two still are in perfect condition. Both are in England, seat of the second industrial revolution: one in Wells, that dates from 1392; and one in Salisbury Cathedral, that has existed, turned and given the hour and the phases of the sun and the moon since

1382. Contemplating in 1972 its toothed wheels, its gears and pulleys, conceived, crafted and put into service more than one hundred years before the discovery of America, I had for the first time the idea of some day writing the book that the reader now has in hand.

The proliferation of mechanical clocks was a manifestation of tendencies that already existed in the culture of the West, and a powerful impulse for the capitalist civilization. The water clocks and sundials of antiquity indicated hours of unequal duration. At the latitude of London, for example, an hour could have from 38 to 82 minutes. But while the West accepted with joy the mechanical clock with all its hours of sixty minutes, a culture as close to the west as the Byzantine Christian culture tenaciously resisted that innovation, equating it to a blasphemy incompatible with the idea of eternity. To this day, orthodox churches do not have clocks in their towers. By contrast, in Western Europe the medieval Catholic Church not only accepted but even sponsored the new way of measuring time. It was from cathedral towers and belfries that the citizens of Florence, Bruges, Paris or London heard, from the fourteenth century, bells announcing a new way of thinking and of channeling and disciplining existence. Lewis Mumford has written of the mechanical clock that it, and not the steam engine, is "the key machine of modern civilization. In each phase of its development, the clock is the most outstanding and the symbol of all machines. Still today there is not such another omnipresent machine. At the beginning of modern technology, there appears, prophetically, the first exact automatic machine destined to make possible in each branch of industrial activity the determination of exact quantities of energy (and therefore standardization), automation, and finally its own product: an exact time. The clock has always maintained its preeminence of all machines. It has a perfection to which the other machines aspire."[5]

By noting such an achievement, we can refute the Third World ideology's convoluted explanations about the causes of the wealth and poverty of nations. We can refer exclusively, if we chose, to the fact that the West was—if not the sole inventor of that paradigmatic machine, the mechanical clock—the fertile ground for its universal adoption and for the lifestyle revolution wrought by social acceptance of the reign (some will say the tyranny) of exactly measured time.

The Case of Oil

We said before that even the raw materials required for the economic activities that led to the growth and prosperity of capitalist civilization were located in the soil of the countries that were protagonists of that civilization. A special, anomalous case that cannot be ignored is the petroleum industry. It began in the United States where to this day there exist immense oil and gas reserves. But the thirst for this new source of energy on the part of an already developed industrial society proved so voracious as to unchain a world struggle for finding and controlling new fields. This gave rise to what is an almost perfect case of the general Third World allegation: by force, by cunning or by bribery, the advanced capitalist countries set about despoiling backward and poor countries of their black gold, easily extracted from the ground, easily handled and transported, in every way superior to coal, and the only fuel appropriate for the internal combustion engine that has played such a decisive role in the capitalist economies of our time. In the means and methods with which the struggle for petroleum was carried out we find an example of the general pattern that supposedly applies to all relations between the advanced capitalist countries and the countries of the Third World: enormous advantage for the former and very little benefit for or outright harm inflicted on the latter.

But it is not fortuitous for the industrialized economies that in cheaply using and exploiting a raw material that they possess in insufficient quantities or completely lack in their own territories, they eventually found that they had fallen into a trap of their own making. The evergrowing comsumption of oil at ridiculously low prices throughout several decades made the industralized countries (not only the capitalist countries, but also the socialist countries without oil reserves, such as East Germany, Czechoslovakia, Poland, Hungary) dependent in the fullest sense of that word. It is primarily from that situation (and only secondarily due to a cartelization that would have quickly fallen apart if it had not been sustained by objective market conditions) that since 1973 the petroleum exporting countries obtained, and will continue to obtain prices that compensate in great part for the unjustly low petroleum prices that prevailed in all of the preceding years. As usually happens, a truly aberrant situation finally found its equilibrium. The capitalist oil importing nations have had to revise their accounts by averaging the cost of all of their purchases of oil, including those made before and those made and still to be made after 1973, and adding to that balance (which is not only economic) their current vulnerability and dependence with relation to ever more precarious sources of supply, as well as perhaps the most serious cost, the distortion of their economies, that were once healthier for their lack of dependence on despoiling overseas territories. The advanced capitalist countries, having benefited during some decades from a subsidy to their economies that in this case was true and tangible, have been converted into semiparasites because of their addiction to cheap petroleum, so that now their major problem is how to overcome the backlash of what appeared, up to 1973, as the clearest and most classic of imperialist advantages.

The fall in petroleum prices since 1982 does not contradict this analysis. OPEC's folly was its behavior in the situation of artificial oil shortage created by the overthrow of the Shah of Iran. Prices above thirty dollars per barrel and speculation above forty dollars in the so-called spot market swiftly forced severe conservation measures: the substitution of petroleum by alternative energy sources such as nuclear power or coal (in December 1981, the equivalent energy of a barrel of petroleum in the form of coal cost ten dollars) and a frenetic exploration resulting in greater oil supply. But the basic situation remains unchanged. Nothing can alter the fact that almost the whole industrial structure and all of the automobiles of the world are designed to use petroleum. Prices will tend to stabilize at a still very high level. And if this stabilization takes place significantly below twenty dollars per barrel, demand will again surge and cause sharp upward fluctuations and unprecedented high prices for oil.

The Case of Agriculture

In recalling the great economic activities that successively have borne the surprising growth, productivity, and prosperity of the capitalist economies, I have mentioned the heavy industries and the high technology industries, the ones that first come to mind as characteristic of the advanced economies. Economists and politicians usually overlook the capitalist activity of greatest growth in productivity, volume, and value of goods produced during the last half century, which is not an industry in the usual sense of the word. Agriculture, the most spectacularly successful capitalist economic activity of the last fifty years, has gone unnoticed by those superficially obsessed by the socialist ideology. The term "agroindustry" has been coined to reconcile this phenomenon with the Marxist prejudice according to which agriculture is a primitive economic activity condemning societies to poverty and backwardness, while machine manufacturing, and above all heavy industry, comprise true progress.

As late as 1900 in the United States half of the labor force was employed in agriculture; in 1945 the proportion was still one-third. By 1983, less than 4 out of every 100 North American workers were employed in agriculture and livestock breeding, and that tiny part of the labor force produced mountains of high-quality food. The contribution of agriculture to the North American GNP, to personal income, to the general welfare and to the economic power of the nation is much greater than simple economic data suggest.

The great productivity of increasingly fewer agriculture workers has caused the liberation of tens of millions of men and women for other occupations more productive, pleasant, and remunerative than farm work had been. And of course, this liberation was in another sense their rescue from what Marx called the cretinism of rural life.

The same has already happened or is rapidly happening in the other advanced capitalist countries, where agriculture has become or is becoming an economic activity characterized by intense capital investment, great technological advance, and an intensive use of automation. The differences in productivity between the advanced capitalist countries and the countries of the Third World (but also the countries called socialist, beginning with the Soviet Union) are much greater in agriculture than in industry. It is normal that a steel mill in a less developed country (as development jargon puts it) should have a productivity of between 30 and 50 percent of the same equipment installed in a developed country. But it is not extraordinary to find differences in a productivity of 10 to 1, or even 25 to 1 between the agriculture of the developed capitalist countries and the agriculture of the countries of the Third World or socialist countries.

Now, in what imaginable way can agriculture and livestock production in the United States, France, Holland, New Zealand, or Canada benefit injustly or abusively by an imperialist relationship between those countries and the Third World? In fact, according to the theory of the unjust international division of labor, with the role of producer and exporter of farm products as supposedly inferior and generating underdevelopment and poverty, the good fortunes of New Zealand and Canada (and Argentina before it was pulled down by Third World ideologists) are inexplicable scandals. Obstinate and dogmatic socialists will perhaps persist in arguing that somehow the sensational yield of agriculture in the countries of advance capitalist economies is another demonstration of how those countries have profited by their exploitation of the Third World. But a nondogmatic, open intelligence will find this additional proof that we are in the presence of societies whose high level of capital accumulation, productivity, and globally satisfactory performance are due to the fact that within a specific historical period (the last six or seven centuries), they have consistently excelled in all fields of human endeavor, whether science, the military, the arts, sports, industry, finance or agriculture. Therefore the advantage that such general skills have undoubtedly and undeniably earned for them in their relations with the present-day Third World—as well as whatever concomitant disadvantage that the latter may have derived from those relations—has been of marginal importance both for the good fortune of the "First World" as for the poor performance of the "Third."

The advanced capitalist countries do not owe their wealth essentially or even in an important or significant way to the no doubt hateful and unjust exactions that they have perpetrated against weaker countries. They were significantly rich and successful before the start of their colonial ventures; and even without them, if there had been only seas where the Third World is, they would have achieved levels of prosperity corresponding to the ingenuity, ambition, and civil virtue of their inhabitants. Capitalist economic expansion received without a doubt a formidable boost with the incorporation of the Third World into the world market, but not exclusively or even importantly through the plunder of those regions. Any gains were made, rather, through the greater dimension of the world market thus achieved.

There was, moreover, a psychologically crucial uplift in the West with the discovery of America and the subsequent exploration of the whole globe by Western navigators, first Spanish and Portuguese and later English, French, and Dutch. But this same example throws light on something so obscured by propaganda and prejudices that it is seldom discussed. Why were the Europeans the discovers of America, and not the other way around? Why, still earlier, did the Europeans travel to the Far East rather than the Chinese to the West? Unleashed in these undertakings were the implicit and latent energies and creative capacities of the West. Exactly the same can be argued of the conquests and the colonization; they were advantageous and in nearly every case benefited the West, but only because previously the West exploded with this energy and creative capacity that in any case would have found expression.

Marx Against the Third World Ideology

In my judgment it is obvious and irrefutable that the rise of rationalism, secularism, the rule of law, political democracy, and the experimental scientific spirit is linked in an organic and inextricable way with the development of capitalist economic systems. If we accept this argument, it cannot be surprising that cultures whose traditions have been alogical or even antilogical, dogmatically religious or even superstitious, tribalist, autocratic, and antiscientific (all fashionable to regard as excellent) have been at least temporarily left behind in a race at which they could not even be present. For these cultures to begin to gain on those who started first, an exceptional effort in the same direction will be necessary, and in fact has been made by several countries, proving that such development is possible.

Let us view in this context the controversy about results in different cultures, of tests designed in the West to measure the intelligence quotient of human beings. As is well known, children (and with more reason, adults) belonging to non-Western cultures, or, within the Western societies, ethnic minorities that adhere only partially to the prevailing values and predominant behavior patterns, achieve lower results in those tests than the "native" children of capitalist civilizations. At first this caused the rational reaction and explanation that the poor achievers in I.Q. tests had not had the cultural advantages that the children of capitalist civilization find in their homes, which are confirmed and reinforced in school and in society. But more recently, in correspondence with the rise of the Third World ideology, this common-sense observation has been overwhelmed and almost silenced by a propagandistic avalanche according to which the values and normal behavior of capitalist civilization are not only not estimable, but are also execrable and infinitely inferior to the values and conduct prevailing in the Third World countries before Western impact and which still determine them as much or more than the traumatic stimulus of Western impact. Therefore, according to the ideology, the countries of the Third World should not be concerned; rather, they should be proud that their children obtain poor results in I.Q. tests designed by and for the natives of capitalist civilization.

I have personally had the opportunity of listening to an Indian anthropologist defiantly explain that there is no reason why the children of India should be expected to solve space-time problems that are often presented in tests measuring intelligence, because the form of seeing and understanding the world of Indian culture is multidimensional and atemporal. This is very respectable but, in view of it and still more extravagant affirmations (such as those of Frantz Fanon on negritude), only by flight from reason and logic can anyone continue giving credibility to the Third World ideology's contention that imperialist exploitation is the explanation for the backwardness and poverty of Asia, Black Africa, and Latin America.

The supposed superiority of non-Western, noncapitalistic societies over the West is to be rejected because it is false and moreover pernicious to the whole world. Every human society is respectable.

The scientists and missionaries of capitalist civilization, incidentally, were the ones who for the first time in history discovered and rejected the limitations and moral blindness of an ethnocentrism that until then had been the norm for all human groups. Having admitted the need to respect and the obligation to understand each ethnic group and culture, we cannot fall into the frivolousness of assigning each one equal weight in the forging of the values, ways and means that could lead mankind toward a more decent, free and prosperous state. Against the contentions of the Third World ideology, the contribution of capitalist civilization has been of an importance that corresponds to its economic superiority. This is not a chance correspondence; rather, one thing is related to the other. I refer, once again, to the Communist Manifesto, and also to the celebration by Marx of the British domination in India. (see chapter 3, note 8).

The Meaning of Modernization

Hardly anyone today dares to be as candid as Marx on the subject of the beneficial influence of the West on the Third World. Condescension, demagogy, and propaganda combine and reinforce each other. The ideology spares the sensitivity of the countries of the Third World (condescension), gains their sympathy (demagogy), or uses them as cannon fodder against the West (propaganda) and thus weaves a network of lies much more alienating for those countries than all of the prejudicial effects that can be attributed to the influence of the West. For example, no one will tell them that the modernization to which they aspire implies their acceptance of a profound transformation in the direction of economic rationality, and the adoption of modern institutions plus the promotion of the social consensus. The West is not specially anxious that such changes take place; it surely would have preferred that non-Western or marginal Western societies should have remain astonished and paralyzed before Western imperial expansion and domination, instead of reacting with diverse degrees of vigor and success, in the way that is now evident and that has eroded and promises to contribute to the end of the Western world hegemony. In each case—from Japan's conversion to capitalist civilization to the other extreme, the blanket adoption of the Third World ideology with its Marxist-Leninst roots and corollaries—it has been backlash against the West that has created the aspiration to modernize. There are those who believe that there is something perverse in the effort to modernize the non-Western or marginal Western countries, to introduce in those societies a dose of rationality, to promote their economic development, their productivity, to raise their standard of living, to give them modern institutions and laws, and to inculcate in the population respect of those laws and institutions and more generally, social discipline. These adversaries of modernization point out, correctly, that all of this is alien to the non-Western countries, and in part also to the marginal Western culture of Latin America. They argue, further, that such conversion to Western values must lead to the loss of identity and soul. It is imperative, they hold, that Asia, Africa, and Latin America turn their backs on modernization according to the model of capitalist civilization, but also (when their objections are consistent) according to the equally Westen model of socialist civilization.

Gunnar Myrdal counters this hatred of modernization. Myrdal charges that it is derived from a particular anthropology inclined to consider any change in a primitive society caused by outside forces as an "intromission." He considers this belief grievously mistaken for various reasons. The traditional values whose perturbation is denounced cannot be the basis of any effective improvement in the societies in question. They are adequate values for a static society, mired in extreme poverty, based on privilege and servitude. When the goal is to rescue a society from a backwardness that inflicts wholesale pain on its members, modernization becomes an imperative, and more so when population growth makes increase in productivity a matter of life or death.[6]

The reader will have noticed that this is essentially the same point that was vigorously held by Marx, but expressed now with caution and somewhat apologetically, instead of being affirmed clearly and without qualms. Such is the confusion that condescension, demagogy and propaganda have introduced, especially since World War II. Yet truth will at times stick its head out, even in the writings of anticapitalists such as Myrdal.

Moreover, behind all of the verbiage about the unique and irreplaceable value of each aspect of non-Western cultures, it is easy to discern an anxious envy of the achievements of capitalist civilization and an anxious desire to emulate them, whether for positive motivations (the aspiration to mitigate poverty and inequality) or for less admirable reasons (the desire to have power, above all military, that flows from technological proficiency). But these desires exist without a full comprehension of how in the advanced capitalist countries those achievements have been the result of a process based on specific social virtues, institutions, and attitudes profoundly rooted in the history and culture of the West.

Condescension, Demagogy, Propaganda

This leads us to the flat statement (derived from common sense and unclouded by condescension, demagogy, or propaganda) that the fundamental cause of poverty and backwardness of the Third World is its original divergence with respect to those social virtues, institutions and attitudes. That way of being, distinct from the way of being of the West, is invariably respectable and can be admirable in many respects, but it is not conducive to the modernization that is desired, and whose frustration the Third World ideology attributes to the wicked operation of causes supposedly foreign and fortuitous. The truth is that in all cases of backwardness and poverty we will find indigenous features of the societies in question, present far prior to all contact with the West, that have acted as dead weights inhibiting the desired and desirable modernization. And this exists within a system of international relations in which some aspects of innovation and modernization have indeed complicated the problems to be overcome in order to achieve a sufficiently global modernization. Moreover, an element of comparison emerges that was absent before: the discovery by masses of people of immensely more attractive possibilities than the severely limited ones to which they have been accustomed produces discouragement and feelings of failure even against the evidence of considerable progress. If one so desires, it is possible to describe this complex of factors as "dependence-imperialism," but with a meaning that is profoundly different from the common one.

Among all of the laborious allegations on the supposedly adverse influence of the West on the present condition of the Third World, the only one that does not stand in opposition to the facts, or is not marginal or insignificant, is the unchaining of the so-called demographic explosion by the universal adoption of Western sanitary practices that have everywhere sharply reduced mortality. Thus an unprecedented demographic pressure has weighed against notable advances in production and productivity (also caused by the West). Except in this area, which is indeed striking, each of the other disadvantages derived by the Third World from its relations with the West either has not in itself been important, or is compensated for by immense advantages that are carefully ignored by the Third World ideology.

For example, there is enormous advantage in having cheap or free access to the constantly growing mass of technical and scientific knowledge accumulated by capitalist civilization. The Third World has had the preferential attention of some of the most fertile minds of the West. It is not for North America that Norman Burlaug developed new varieties of cereals with high yields, but rather for the undernourished masses of Southeast Asia and India. In seeking modernization, the countries of the Third World have the advantage of emulating the successes and avoiding the errors of the pioneers of capitalist civilization. Repeatedly, countries that have had to act in this way have in their turn succeeded. These include nineteenth century Germany to twentieth century Japan, countries that have not committed the folly of investing scarce resources in declining industries but have concentrated on rising ones or areas where they could compete advantageously. It is hardly imputable to the advanced capitalist countries (rather, it can be blamed on the influence of the socialist spirit with its mania for privileging heavy industry) that the Third World tends to disregard the lessons of an open book, and insists on having steel mills instead of turning to areas where it enjoys comparative advantages. Of course, frequently it will be found that these latter are complementary to the world capitalist economy—tourism, for example, or light industry designed for export to advanced capitalist countries—which makes them repugnant to the Third World ideology. This is mainly why governments of that tendency do not preferentially undertake the development of areas of economic activity where their countries have comparative advantages, and even go to the extreme of discouraging or destroying those economic activities that such governments find already thriving when they come to power, as in the example of Michael Manley and the tourist industry in Jamaica.

Nevertheless, hardly anyone perceives or, perceiving it, is ready to acknowledge the enormous responsibility of socialism in the frustrations of the Third World. Yet almost everybody has been infected by the Third World ideology and finds nothing short of axiomatic the arbitrary assertion that something in the capitalist system is the only hindrance, or in any case the greatest obstacle for the development and happiness of the Third World.

UNCTAD, the North-South Dialogue and the Brandt Commission

The opinion is frequently expressed that in any case the rich countries could pull the Third World out of its backwardness, if they at least were to fulfill the recommendations that UNCTAD (United Nations Conference on Trade and Development) has accumulated over the years. The bulk of these recommendations hold that trade between the rich and the poor should be based not on reciprocity, but on concessions of the rich countries[7] in favor of the poor countries. It is sensibly affirmed that if the result were the take-off of the latter the whole world would benefit, because of the greater volume of wealth produced and traded, and even more important, the decrease in the grave and growing tensions caused by international inequality. As early as 1968 at a meeting in New Delhi, UNCTAD defined areas of possible action, including better and more stable prices for the raw materials that the Third World exports to the developed world; more unconditional or less restricted openings of the markets of the developed world to manufactured products from the Third World; and nonrefundable financial assistance, such as a system of "soft" loans, as well as measures tending to lighten the considerable burden of debt for Third World countries vis-à-vis the advanced capitalist countries.

The recommendations of UNCTAD have since been the object of intense debate, for example in the so-called North-South Dialogue which, according to its most optimistic advocates, should lead to a "new international economic order." The 1981 Brandt Commission (after its chairman, former German chancellor Willy Brandt) included not only dogmatic Third World ideologues but also prominent European conservatives such as former British prime minister Edward Heath. The Commission did not hesitate to subscribe final recommendations and warnings that called for affirmative action to remedy the imminently trouble-provoking problem of the inequality of nations.[8]

The Brandt Commission essentially followed in the footsteps of UNCTAD with some additional recommendations: to channel part of the resources presently invested in arms toward the development of the poor countries; to stop the export of arms to the Third World; to battle world hunger and disease; to create a stabilizing fund to protect raw material producers from catastrophic price fluctuations; to promote more generous and less costly financing of development projects in the Third World by the World Bank and the International Monetary Fund with money from the North; and to encourage more participation by the poor countries if not in the operations (for which they lack the means) at least in the benefits of the common patrimony of mankind, such as high seas fishing or the exploitation of the minerals in the ocean floor.

Some of the demands of the UNCTAD, some of the proposals of the South to the North, some of the recommendations of the Brandt Commission are feasible and should be implemented, leaving aside the futile debate about the supposed obligation of a transfer of wealth, due as compensation for a supposed previous injury, that the industrialized countries should effect in favor of the poor and backward countries.

The Limits of International Social Justice

What the West must reject, since it would be tantamount to psychological and political defeat (sure forerunners of eventual Soviet world domination) is the role assigned to it by the Third World ideology of being criminally guilty of having caused all of the misfortunes of the Third World. Such rejection of false guilt by the West does not mean ignoring what I have called the international social question. The West should listen to the just claims of the Third World, but also to the unjust, on condition that they are not hopelessly conflictive (and designed intentionally to be so). Some of those claims seem to be or are indeed excessive. But that was also the case not so long ago of the claims of the workers through their unions in the advanced capitalist countries. The meetings of those demands by a process of negotiation and bargaining has resulted in less damage to society than the violent conflicts that were the alternative.

Moreover, who can say when a demand for national or international social justice is excessive, so that yielding to it would result in more harm than good? This can be said more or less with certainty of those demands whose transparent purpose is to damage the very fabric of capitalist civilization, with the objective of bringing about its descruction and substitution by socialism. In Europe, where a very important part of the labor movement until World War II was conducted with that strategic goal in mind, the mobilization of the working class had almost uniformly deplorable results. Salaries remained low, methods of production archaic, and finally some democratic political systems ceased resisting the destructive onslaughts of a labor movement more interested in unleashing revolution than in winning material advantages for the workers, and which for that reason pressed deliberately conflictive claims. In contrast, the North American labor movement had the luck of getting away early from the control of doctrinaire socialists and anarchists, and turned instead to improving the material conditions of workers. The ensuing relentless union pressure for shorters hours, higher real wages and better working conditions in great part explains the "natural selection" among American entrepreneurs that resulted in the elimination of the incompetents and the Malthusians, in favor of the innovators and the visionaries. In this way, "excessive" demands by the labor sector of the North American economy, far from weighing it down, prodigiously stimulated it, forcing it to leave behind semihandicraft, restrictive, Malthusian methods of production that continued for a long time in Europe, as part of the frantic search for the way to pay more for fewer hours of work thorough managerial and technological advance and mass production. This is what characterized the great North American industrial expansion and caused the amazement and the envy of the whole world. Perhaps the developed capitalist world faces a similar challenge and opportunity with relation to the Third World, and should not out of hand reject as excessive all Third World claims.

The consequences of rejection can be imagined if we realize that even putting into effect in the short term all of the sensible and feasible recommendations (because there are some that are extravagant or impossible) of, say, the Brandt Commission, does not guarantee, to say the least, the happy resolution of the international social question. In fact, even if we suppose that all of the demands of UNCTAD be met, the problem of the backwardness and poverty of the Third World would not therefore be solved as long as the Third World ideology remains influential.

Now, there is an intense interest on the part of those who wish to destroy capitalist civilization that the Third World should not free itself from the paralyzing effect of that ideology and turn toward rationality for the solution or the alleviation of its problems. What Third World ideologists seek and have so far achieved is that poor and backward countries should remain so, and continue to accumulate frustration and resentment against the developed capitalist world. Thus the socialist infection has made large parts of the Third World even more resistant than before to political and economic rationality.

Notes

1. I refer in what follows to Jean Gimpel, *La Revolution Industrielle du Moyen Age* (Paris: Seuil, 1975), pp. 5-7, 9, 14, 18, 141-60.
2. Ibid.
3. Ibid.
4. Ibid.
5. Lewis Mumford, *Technics and Civilization* (New York: Harcourt Brace Jovanovich, 1963), quoted by Jean Gimpel, *La Revolution Industrielle*, p. 142.
6. Gunnar Myrdal, *The Challenge of World Poverty* (Middlesex: Penguin, 1970), pp. 42-45.
7. This refers to advanced capitalist ones. Countries such as the Soviet Union and East Germany are excluded from the classification of "rich" without any justification since, while it is true that they have a poor output in relation to their resources (the Soviet Union) or to the exceptional productive capacity of their populations (East Germany) they could contribute to the economy of the Third World to an extent at least comparable to the value of the military investment they make there. But they excuse themselves with the argument (of no moral value, even if it were not false) that

they owe nothing to the Third World, because they did not cause its poverty and backwardness, as the advanced capitalist countries supposedly did. It would therefore fall exclusively upon these latter to economically aid the Third World. This means that the United States supposedly had the obligation to aid (as in fact it did until April, 1981) the Marxist government of Nicaragua, while the Soviet Union specialized in arming that government and using its Nicaraguan connection to stir up civil war in neighboring El Salvador.

8. The Conference of Cancún, in October 1981, was the direct result of the Brandt Commission Report.

8

Wealth and Poverty of Nations, II

So-called development literature reached and still largely holds a virtual unanimity in attributing the backwardness and poverty of the Third World—but also frequently the progress and prosperity of the advanced capitalist countries—to the relationship between the two: to imperialism and its corollary, dependence. There was (and there persists, because without it the Third World ideology would collapse) a strange lack of historical and cultural perspective when explaining the wealth and poverty of nations. A hypothesis that is not contemplated holds that one of the principal factors that should be taken into account to explain the differences between the countries of the earth is the great cultural variety and geographic environment of the diverse human societies such as they were before the first contact between them. Among other anomalies, that abstraction of some of the most fundamental facts of the problem has allowed the presumed development experts to argue the following nonsense: On the one hand, they assure us that the development of the advanced capitalist countries is an aberration and is parasitical ("it wouldn't have been possible without the despoiling of the Third World"); on the other hand they suggest— or resolutely affirm—that only the despoiling activity of imperialism and the dead weight of dependence, that is, external, contingent, and recent factors, have impeded a similar and even superior development in the countries that continue to be poor and backward.

On such a transparent fallacy have been constructed impressive dialectic buildings, whose true sustenance is not facts but rather the necessity to keep alive the propagandistic and proselytizing value of the Third World ideology. One can go from generalizations to particular demonstrations of how some supposedly well-formulated (rarely the case) goal of an Asian, African or South American country has been frustrated by the mechanisms of imperialism and dependence. For the sake of that demonstration, careful abstraction is made of the fact that such mechanisms, to the degree that they in effect operate in the described form, require, to be operational (for example, by the corruption of officials) a prior vulnerability on the part of the social body, comparable to low defenses in an organism, making it unable to resist the attack of viruses and bacteria. No one in his right mind would dream of affirming that the sick, if they could have remained in a sterile environment without social intercourse of any kind, would not only stay healthy, but would moreover be olympic champions.

Asian Drama

Although submerged by propaganda, however, the truth cannot be totally annihilated, and it rears its head in the most unexpected ways. Gunnar Myrdal was one of the most influential cultivators of the spurious thesis according to which the capitalist West is in some way responsible for the backwardness of the Third World.[1] But in recent years professor Myrdal has had the intellectual honesty to revise that aspect of his convictions, although not his obsession with central planning, eventually coercive, as the best route toward the development of the poor countries. The illumination of professor Myrdal in regard to the real causes of poverty had its origin in his extensive and profound investigation of Southeast Asia. The result was his monumental three-volume work, *Asian Drama* and a corollary in the form of the shorter book, *The Challenge of World Poverty*. This latter volume is a true mine of succinct and penetrating observations which, together, form a devastating critique of the most common and most generally accepted premises and affirmations of the Third World ideology.[2]

Myrdal shows in the most explicit and categorical way that the literature on development, in vogue from 1945 on, glosses over most distinctive characteristics of the poor and backward countries that are to a great degree responsible both for their backwardness and for the difficulties they find in attempting to overcome it. Those characteristics consist above all of "non-economic factors, broadly attitudes and institutions of such paramount importance that they cannot be abstracted from in economic theory and in planning."[3] Those attitudes and institutions are traditional and preceded all contact with the capitalist West. On the other hand, they are not comparable (as the proponents of the development literature argue, when they include in a single category all preindustrial societies) to the attitudes and institutions that prevailed in today's advanced capitalist countries when they were agrarian societies.

Myrdal writes:

> Conditions in underdeveloped countries raise much stronger inhibitions (among those in power) and obstacles (among the masses of people) to development than in the developed countries. . . . In regard to attitudes and institutions . . . this would hold true even if a comparison were made to the developed countries at an earlier time when they were undergoing their industrial revolutions or even in previous centuries. . . . In regard to political institutions, one obvious difference is that the now developed countries . . . well before their industrial revolutions . . . formed a small world of broadly similar cultures, within which people and ideas circulated rather freely. . . . In this small world, long before the industrial revolution, rationalism had been fostered and traditionalism weakened as the Renaissance, the reformation and the Enlightenment successively revolutionized concepts and valuations. Modern scientific thought developed in these countries and a modernized technology began early to be introduced in their agriculture and their industries, which at that time were all small-scale.[4]

Today's prosperous and advanced countries early achieved (and propagated among the colonies they populated, the United States, Canada, Australia, New Zealand) a social cohesion, an organic set of motivations and an effective solidarity that permitted them to pursue and meet important collective goals even before their differentiation into independent nation-states and much before their industrialization. They formed, as Myrdal remarks, a compact world (Western Christendom, as Toynbee puts it) of homogeneous culture within which people and ideas circulated freely and so did the first machines—including that paradigm of all machines, the mechanical clock (see chapter 7). In that compact, homogeneous, and dynamic world, much before the industrial revolution, rationalism had made decisive advances and pushed back nonrational motivations.

None of this is especially novel or remarkable, but that Gunnar Myrdal should take note of it! Development literature does not normally give the least attention to cultural differences that are clearly the principal explanation for the inequalities that persist between nations. To recognize this would be to throw off that literature which aims to flatter the "new countries," reinforcing in them the obsession that they are free from responsibility for their backwardness, and to persuade them that the only special effort they must make to escape poverty is to get cash in compensation for the supposed harm that has been done to them by the West—or better still, break away from the West through socialist revolution.

The Influence of Climate

Myrdal topples another shibboleth when he makes the banal observation, but unusual in the context of the development literature, that climate is another difference of great importance when comparing the developed and backward countries. Almost all of the latter are situated in tropical or subtropical zones, while so far all the cases of successful modernization have occurred in the temperate zones. "This cannot be entirely an accident of history, but must have to do with some special handicaps, directly or indirectly related to climate."[5] Again professor Myrdal is not saying anything especially original or profound, but he must be credited with departing from the strange inhibition in the development literature before such an obvious and enormous fact. He adds that little research has been carried out about the importance of climate conditions in development planning. It is clear, nevertheless, that the extremes of heat and humidity in most underdeveloped countries contribute to a deterioration of soil and many kinds of material goods; bear a partial responsibility for the low productivity of certain crops; explain why certain crops, forests and animals cannot thrive in these regions; and not only cause discomfort to workers, but also impair their health and decrease participation in and duration of work and its efficiency.

The inhibition of the development literature on the subject of climate is actually not surprising. It stems from the shared victory of the two superpowers in World War II and their resulting consensus on the absolute harm that the European colonial expansion had caused. The development literature, to which the United Nations and its specialized agencies made a decisive contribution, was constructed on the mistaken foundation of that indiscriminate reproof, naive and devoid of special purpose on the part of the United States, astute and intentional on the part of the Soviet Union. It became virtually unthinkable in international agencies and Western universities to dedicate funds, approve plans of action or of research, employ experts or professors, or even give good grades to students who had the bad taste to suggest that there could be any other explanation than imperialism and colonial rule for the backwardness of what at that time began to be called the "Third World." Climate is blind and neutral; to have taken it into consideration would have been to admit that the problem of backwardness in some regions of the world cannot be explained principally or entirely by the words imperialism, colonialism, and dependence.

The Influence of Disease

The variables that it would be necessary to consider to untangle the problem of the historical diversity of human groups are enormously complex and of extremely remote origin. This is powerfully conveyed in William H. McNeill's *Plagues and People* (1977), a study of the impact of infectious diseases in history.[6]

Until recently the way diseases spread was totally unknown. The discoveries of the tuberculosis bacillus and of anthrax by Koch and Pasteur were as late as 1877 and 1879, respectively. Until 1892 the great city of Hamburg did not do anything to supply its residents with uncontaminated water. The municipal government did not believe in the existence of little invisible animals, until in the year mentioned above a cholera epidemic visited all the houses on the Hamburg side of the street that divides Hamburg from Altona, and none of the houses on the other side, supplied by a different water source run by the government of Prussia.

That disorientation of scientists with relation to the cause of infectious diseases caused the corresponding lack of understanding in historians about the economic, political, social, and psychological consequences of epidemics and of endemic infections. In our own time, used as we are to living in societies that enjoy unprecedented good health, even the most penetrating historians have persisted in paying little attention to and considering as exaggerated, exceptional, insignificant, within the complex of factors that have determined the evolution of human societies, the report of massive death by epidemic disease. Not even the epidemic of bubonic plague that between 1347 and 1350 killed a third of the population of Europe has received comparable attention to, say, the Hundred Years' War, in spite of the fact that the so-called Black Death left a much more profound imprint on the art and literature of the West, which suggests that the plague was from every point of view more important than the war. And surely the even greater influence of endemic diseases has gone practically unnoticed. And this, McNeill tells us is in spite of the fact that epidemics and endemic infections have always been and will again be decisive in history.

The idea of investigating this subject came to the author while pondering the unbelievable conquest of Mexico by Cortés at the head of a handful of Spaniards, but also the still more surprising cultural conquest of the immense territory between California and the Tierra del Fuego by no more than thirty thousand Spaniards in less than one hundred years. Why did the Precolumbian religions of Mexico and Peru disappear without a trace? How can it be explained that civilized people, owners of a complex culture, did not conserve at least a clandestine memory and their attachment to gods and rites that immemorially had guaranteed the fertility of their fields and their women? Such questions could not occur to the Spaniards, to whom it seemed that the massive accepance of baptism and of the Catholic faith by the conquered Amerindians was natural and evidently due to the fact that it was the true religion.

But given the demise of such native ethnocentrism the whole episode must be revised in a new light.[7]

The Psychological Surrender

The basic explanation offered by McNeill is not in itself novel. It was known, and has been mentioned as one of the causes for the defeat of Aztecs, that they were victims of eruptive diseases the origins of which were unknown to them, and lethal among them although common and generally harmless among the invaders. In the moment of the "sad night" (just after the great defeat of Cortés) a smallpox epidemic was decimating Tenochtitlan, and probably because of that fact the Spaniards were not pursued and annihilated.

To the knowledge of those facts that existed McNeill adds first the hypothesis that the loss of life through sickness must have been much greater than has been imagined until now. There are no modern examples of the meeting of numerous and densely established human populations with previously unknown viruses and bacteria, but we might gain insight by examining an animal population that met that fate in 1950. We have very precise observations made on the population of rabbits in Australia from the moment when the mixomatosis virus was carried there deliberately to stop the explosive and prejudicial proliferation of the rabbits (a species brought for the first time into Australia ninety years earlier). The result, completely unforeseen, was that in just one year the infection spread over an area comparable to that of Europe, killing 998 of each 1,000 rabbits. The following year the mortality rate for survivors dropped to 90 percent; Seven years later, it dropped to 25 percent.

The most critical point, when the rabbit population was almost extinct, occurred three years after the beginning of the epidemic. Because the number of generations of rabbits occurring in three years equals between ninety and one-hundred years of human generations, it is possible to suspect that the Amerindians may have needed nearly a century or more to begin to recover from the initial impact of infections brought by the Spaniards, as unknown in America before 1492 as mixomatosis in Australia before 1950.

But even if we suppose a much smaller death toll, another factor enters that by itself would help explain the apparently inexplicable submission of the Amerindians to the European conquerors. The Aztecs, Incas, and other American natives not only were ravaged and debilitated by new diseases, but perhaps more important, could find no other explanation than the desertion or defeat of their gods for the magical partiality of the infections against them in favor of the Spaniards. They must have concluded that the gods (the culture) of the invaders were superior. This psychological surrender had to have much more profound and lasting consequences than a simple military defeat.

The Origin of Development

These explanations, no doubt satisfactory for this particular case, lead to a more fundamental question. Where and how did the Spaniards obtain the relative immunity to certain infectious diseases that served them so well in their confrontation with the Amerindians, making it surely their best weapon? In search of the answer, McNeill discovers an unsuspected dimension of history. We become persuaded that infectious diseases and their geographic distribution have had a multiple and profound impact on human affairs. Among a variety of other questions, that of the influence of climate on the diverse fortune of human societies is sharply underlined. McNeill goes much farther than the obvious observation that extremes of heat and humidity are impediments to human action. He develops the hypothesis that upon leaving behind the humid tropical jungle that was the original habitat of hominoids and of the first true men, certain small human groups rid themselves of a large number of parasites and other infectious agents that persist in being the bane of tropical regions. Where infectious microorganisms were no longer a crushing burden, human intelligence, liberated for the first time, could be employed in subduing and taming nature. This occurred in the valley of the Nile, at the same time dry and irrigated by the river; in Mesopotamia; in the river valleys of China; and eventually, with maximum effect, in what is today Europe. The health and life expectancy of those fugitives from the humid jungle improved, and as a consequence, they proliferated. This success generated new problems and challenges, and also new creative responses. The inhabitants of the humid jungles or of the African grass plain had been exclusively gatherers of wild fruits and hunters, a combination of the food-gathering ways of monkeys and lions. Larger human agglomerations had to turn to less random and more productive methods, and finally to the cultivation of plants and the domestication of animals. Committed now definitively to civilization, men from then until the present time have found themselves forced to incessant efforts of economic, social, and political creativity. To begin with, structures that were still primitive (those of the Neolithic period) but that had achieved a high level of demographic density, were therefore exposed to universal contagion of what today we call "childhood diseases," and in time reached an ecological balance with them. "When civilized societies learned to live with diseases that can only persist among large human populations, they acquired a very potent biological weapon [which] came into play whenever new contacts with previously isolated human groups occurred."[8]

Neolithic, and later civilized societies, rapidly achieved a complexity and productivity incomparable to life in the humid jungle and were, for that reason, very vulnerable to alien aggression. The necessity of enhancing the capacity to resist that ever-present threat was the principal stimulus to political organization. And that has been, perhaps, the main stimulus, throughout history, of what we call development. The absence of a comparable context confirms the etiology of the backwardness that still prevails today in societies which, moreover, have the misfortune of remaining in the same regions of unhealthy and ennervating climate in which their primitive ancestral societies vegetated.

The Soft State

Once he was persuaded that the factors keeping a large part of humanity in backwardness and poverty have their roots, principally, in the original state of these regions before contact with the West, Gunnar Myrdal coined the expression "soft state" to characterize those societies. What is involved is not that the typical Third World state be benign. Very much to the contrary, too often it is authoritarian and tyrannical. Myrdal refers to the fact that it tends to be only a caricature of the nation-states of the West, and that, as a consequence, it does not work. The so-called soft state has no social solidarity or discipline. There prevails a generalized tolerance for corruption, and a lack of respect for or simple lack of comprehension of legal systems more-or-less copied from the West. Lack of social discipline and disrespect for the law are not exclusive to the masses of the poor and uneducated, but also prevail among the elites. Public officials at all levels tend to neglect or to distort instructions received from higher levels, which themselves tend to be incompetent, cynical and corrupt. Graft, extortion, embezzlement, and bribery prevail. Taxes, to the degree that they exist, are evaded with impunity, and tolerance of arbitrary and irregular practices are taken advantage of by those who have social, economic or political power, frequently accumulated in the same individuals. Just as corruption is tolerated, low performance, nonfulfillment of goals, and lack of punctuality are normal. "All those countries independent of their type of government, have in general placed many fewer obligations much less effectively upon their peoples than have Western countries." [9]

State control, which Third World countries adopted with such enthusiasm under the influence of the British socialist spirit has had the unexpected effect of prodigiously stimulating corruption. Each control, each regulation, each license, each permit is an impediment to economic activity, removable only by bribes, kickbacks, and other forms of corruption. The tendency is that in some way this invisible tax is always being paid. Purchases made by governments are routinely subject to overpricing, destined to enrich high civil or military officials.

Myrdal reaches a devastating conclusion: "While on the one hand, it has proved difficult in underdeveloped countries to introduce rational profit motives and market behavior into the sector of life where they operate in developed countries—that is, the sphere of business; it has, on the other hand, proved equally difficult to eliminate motives of private gains in the sector where they have been largely suppressed in the developed countries—the sphere of public responsibility and power."[10] Is this the consequence of imperialism and dependence? Myrdal answers: We have here "remnants of the traditional and precapitalist society. Where there are no markets or where those that exist are exceedingly imperfect, 'connections' have to be substituted." [11] This implies a fragmentation of loyalties, in particular little loyalty toward the community, whether it be at the local level or the national level. The position of power exploitable for one's private benefit can be very high, such as that of a minister whose consent is required to effect a large transaction; or it can be very low, such as that of a petty official who can delay or impede a permit, the use of a railway car or the opportune opening of the gates over the tracks. Indonesia, for example, enjoyed as a Dutch colony an almost total absence of corruption, but with independence in a few years the public administration became totally corrupt, and the explanation for this change has to be looked for in "the legacy from traditional society."[12]

The Levels of Underdevelopment

Asian Drama and *The Challenge of World Poverty* refer to Southeast Asia, to countries such as Indonesia, Burma, India, Pakistan, and Sri Lanka. But all those who have firsthand knowledge of one or several of the other societies that, not by chance, conform to the Third World, will recognize with sadness in Myrdal's books the characteristic features, to a lesser or greater degree, of each one of those countries.

A brief reflection will lead us to admit that some of the countries characterized as imperialist, for the sole reason that they are Western and not communist, share many of the same features of the underdeveloped countries identified by Myrdal. These include Italy, Spain, Portugal and Greece, the least successful and most Third World–like of European countries. And even within countries, the frontiers between the regions that had the vocation of development, and for that reason have achieved it, and those that were culturally inclined to remain backward and poor, can be clearly discerned. The Third World ideology might argue that Lombardy and Catalonia are rich because the Italian Mezzogiorno and Andalucia are poor, when it is truer that, in many ways, the prosperity and progress of the former have served to mitigate the backwardness and poverty of the latter.

What Everybody Knows

The Third World ideology flourishes in books and articles, speeches and political documents, in debates at international assemblies, or in sermons in the political arena; the Third World ideologue, in a polemic, will modulate his voice or sharpen his pen to pour fire and brimstone on imperialism and dependence as fundamental causes of differences among nations. But in private, the true opinion of the same individual might manifest itself, for example, in complaints about the untrustworthiness of his servant because of her nationality, contradictorily with praises for her reliability *in spite of* her nationality. Thus when he is really speaking his mind, our Third World ideologue will say what the whole world knows (and what professor Myrdal, exceptionally, admits in his study on Southeast Asia): that the uneven fortunes of countries are essentially due to the people who inhabit them. For the purposes of the Third World ideology, an abstraction is made of cultural differences, and Bangladesh is discussed as if it were an entity entirely comparable to Switzerland, except for the fact that the Bengalis have suffered from imperialism and the Swiss have taken advantage of it. The reasons (some of them very easily discernible, such as climate, and others more complex) that make the Swiss as a human group more competent than the Bengalis (and this from long before any European set foot in Bengal) need to be studied and understood, and surely more seriously and sincerely than is usually the case in the development literature. But it is a transparent sham to ignore the prima facie evidence that there exist enormous cultural differences between the Swiss and the Bengalis, and that those differences are more than sufficient to explain the very distinct fortunes of the two countries.

> Max Thurn has formulated this in the most blunt possible way: "Are there really rich and poor countries? With regard to natural resources, such is undoubtedly the case. Some countries have fertile land and mineral deposits. Others have only land and rocky mountains. Then, are the first rich and the latter poor? Think of Bolivia with its tin mines, its oil wells and its fertile low lands. Think of Argentina with its plains covered by more than a meter of humus and its benign climate. Think of Indonesia. There is little that nature has denied of those countries. And nevertheless they are poor. On the contrary Switzerland, that has no natural resources of any kind, is the rich of the rich. Wealth does not depend on natural resources, it depends on man . . . To perceive this, it is sufficient to imagine the transplantation of 50 million Indonesians to Germany (or, for that matter, to France) and of 50 million Germans (or French) to Indonesia. Which would be the rich country and which would be the poor country in a period of ten years?"[13]

The Case of Israel

The imaginative effort that Max Thurn proposes is unnecessary. Reality gives us the case of Israel, the surprising result of a fairly similar experiment. And the argument is void that Israel has benefited from an immense foreign aid, since Israel has had to invest the greater part of that aid in armaments and in the military training of its population. (Each young Israeli must interrupt his studies for two years to serve in the armed forces, and each citizen must quit his regular work for two months of the year for the same reason.) And consider that all the foreign aid given to Israel falls far short of what the Arab countries and other petroleum exporters have received and continue to receive in exchange for their natural wealth.

Israel is a country that has been made cohesive due to the permanent threat of its neighbors. Yet even within Israel we see a problem in the split between the European segment of society and the underdeveloped segment of Middle Eastern or North African origin (Sephardim). These latter constitute "another" Israel; they are the objects of enormous effort by leaders to raise them to the level of the Israelis of European origin. The problem is perceived as a matter of life and death for the state. Over ten years ago, the Hebrew University of Jerusalem established a special tuition-free school to prepare young Sephardic people for admission into higher education. The percentage of Sephardic students in the university has only risen from 11 to less than 20 percent, a dissapointing result. And students whose families come from the Middle East and North Africa leave the university before graduation much more frequently than their counterparts of European origin.

The armed forces confront a similar problem. Israel's armed forces are probably the most hungry for human resources and therefore the most impartial in the world. Yet almost all of the pilots of the Israeli air force must be recruited from the Ashkenazim (Jews of European origin). David Ben-Gurion used to say that his dream was to find a Jew of Middle Eastern or African origin capable of being chief of staff. For that purpose he founded a special school headed by the best professors, to provide optimal military training for selected young Sephardim. Yet, years later, the majority of the graduates had not passed beyond the rank of staff sergeant.

The Israeli experience with that part of its population whose culture, wholly Jewish, is nevertheless conditioned by centuries of residence in the Middle East and in North Africa offers discouraging short-term prospects for the Third World. Israel's Sephardim come from Turkey, Syria, Iraq, Iran, Egypt, Yemen, Tunisia, Algeria, Morocco, countries far more fortunate than regions almost entirely deprived of a cultural base, like equatorial Africa. If Israel has had difficulty in pulling up its Sephardim, how much more difficult will it be for countries suffering underdevelopment that have nothing comparable to Israel's Ashkenazi base; who persist in being overwhelmed by the same complex of physical factors, such as climate, and cultural disadvantages that are at the origin of their poverty and backwardness; and that have in recent years been disoriented and intoxicated by the Third World ideology. It will take a very different kind of revolution from the one socialists propose for those countries to find within themselves the spiritual and intellectual resources indispensible to the exorcism of their phantoms—confronting their true problems and setting about wholeheartedly to join capitalist civilization.

When Nothing Succeeds like Failure

We have seen the immense collision of the West with other civilizations, all of which, without exception, were more or less lacking in scientific and technological vocation, and all of which were in decline (those of the Old World) or immature (those of the New World) at the time of that collision. The result has been a fragmentation of those civilizations into caricatures of the nation-states of the West, with almost all of their defects and very few of their virtues. Within each of those nation-states, the most apt and ambitious individuals, previously frustrated and embittered by the racism and the exclusiveness of the Europeans, have today gained positions of leadership. At first they did not face the problem of legitimacy. They had been martyrs in the struggle for independence and with its arrival, national heroes. They were the Nehrus, Nassers, Sukarnos, Kenyattas, and Ben Bellas. These founding fathers, none of them competent administrators and all obsessed by the Third World ideology, tragically overestimated both the harm of colonialism and the advantage of independence.[14]

The second generation (Mobutu instead of Lumumba, Suharto instead of Sukarno, Indira Gandhi instead of Nehru) in addition finds itself overwhelmed by the consequences of bad economic decisions made by their predecessors. Their defensive and so far politically successful response, has been an overdose of the same bad medicine: an overdose of Third World ideology. And why not? Their experience has been that no matter how economically inept, they gain international prestige and strengthen their power to the same degree that they loudly trumpet the Third World ideology. And those who refuse to play the game risk the loss of their honor, their position, and even their lives, as did President Sadat of Egypt.

To be enshrined as a good Third World ideologue, one must declare oneself socialist, adopt and proclaim the hypothesis that the problems of the poor countries are wholly due to colonialism, neocolonialism, imperialism and dependence, show hostility toward the West (especially the United States) and a prejudice toward—or frank adherence to—the Soviet Union. It is also necessary to adopt and put into practice governmental measures antagonistic to the market economy, as did Michael Manley in Jamaica. There is usually nothing to lose by it, unless, as in Jamaica, the Third World ideology has still not managed to destroy political democracy. In the absence of elections that Third World ideologues might lose, these leaders achieve the ruin of their countries with impunity, carrying them to levels of poverty, tyranny, disorganization, personal insecurity and corruption not even imaginable a few years ago, when they were not yet independent. The population will have no possible redress against this catastrophe.

And there will be no loss of prestige in the world, and less in the West than in anywhere else because of its overabundance of Third World ideologues, apologists for any Manley or Mengistu, or even Idi Amin Dada. In the universities of the West we invariably find apologists ready to hold that such demagogues or tyrants are beyond reproach as nationalist or even socialist leaders, and that any and all misfortunes suffered by the peoples they rule are a direct consequence of past and present Western sins.

In 1980, as Uganda was ravaged by famine in the aftermath of a Tanzanian invasion, Jean-François Revel expressed his amazement at the virtual immunity from criticism and automatic exoneration enjoyed by the worst Third World leaders despite their cruelty and incompetence: "When unemployment or inflation in Western countries are discussed, these things are regarded as the consequence of acts of government and not as the result of blind fate . . . The economic failure of communist (western) countries, say Poland, is rightly attributed to inept or wrong policies. But incompetence or dishonesty in government are abstracted in the case of Third World Countries. Why? because we are friends of the Third World? friends, rather, of the tyrants of the Third World. It is strange that the woes of Third World peoples should elicit only indifference except when they can be blamed on the West."[15] Actually, Revel was understating his case. The famine in Ethiopia which coincided with Mengistu's $150 million celebration of the first ten years of his rule, was caused entirely by his policies. Third World ideologists have tried to blame it on the West.

Probable Consequences of Third World Ideology Infection

The few countries of the Third World where democracy survives are not safe from the Third World ideology infection. The Third World ideologue, with his bias toward state interventionism and his paranoia about the economic mechanisms of capitalism, aims at increasing the powers of the state and assumes and fosters a defensive attitude and xenophobia against the world market. The invariable result is a politicization of all fields of human activity and an anemia of civil society. In

India, Mexico or Venezuela no citizen, no matter how productive and worthy, is sure of his position in society unless he has taken care to establish close links with politicians, an indispensable step to avoid being the victim of abuses of power. Such a citizen, who in more propitious circumstances would have devoted all of his or her energy to fulfilling the proper social role of entrepreneur, will have to negotiate privileges with the political class or even take on a full-time political role.

Let us not lose sight, finally, of the fact that a decisive part of the vigor and virulence of the Third World ideology, in spite of its being a transparent fraud, is directly due to the existence and the actions of the Soviet Union. Since its beginnings in 1917 the influence of the socialist camp has been powerful, stemming from the fascination of socialism itself, and from the accident of history when Marxist radicals, the Leninists, managed to grab hold of the world's largest country, the one most well endowed with natural resources, and with one of the most numerous, most traditionally submissive and at the same time courageous and resilient populations of the planet. In the years since 1917, that first socialist state has become rigidly conservative domestically but, paradoxically, in order to maintain its legitimacy before its own people and to increase its world influence (two faces of the same coin) it must persist in acting subversively in the international scene, where it promotes revolts, revolutions, civil wars, and terrorist acts provided that the structures so assailed are in some way meshed with the economic, political, and military machinery, or with the social and moral fabric of the West. If this requirement is met, there is no psychopathic assassin, mad bomber or tyrant too repulsive to be excluded from the multiple advantages of Soviet benevolence. Moreover, the beneficiaries of the Soviet connection do not risk the mistrust or open hostility of all leaders of the West; they do not risk the loss of sympathetic progressive opinion in Europe and the United States that finds in the Third World ideology its amusement and its alibi.

Given this, the existence and survival of African, Asian and Latin American political leaders who do not render sincere or opportunistic homage to the Third World ideology is an anomaly. Yet those holdouts exist, and in very recent times they are getting more of a hearing as the universal failure of the Third World ideology becomes ever more apparent. Such leaders, if they were ever to become the wave of the future, would be the ones to pull their countries from backwardness and rescue them from neurosis by liberating the enormous latent force of the market economy.

But this remains a hopeful speculation. What seems to be in the cards is that the majority of the countries of the Third World will pass through a stage of falling prey to some form of authoritarianism or totalitarianism parading under the banner of socialism.

Notes

1. For example, Gunnar Myrdal, *Development and Underdevelopment* (Cairo, 1956)
2. Gunnar Myrdal, *Asian Drama,* 3 vols. (London: Pelican, 1968); and idem, *The Challenge of World Poverty* (London: Pelican, 1970).
3. Myrdal, *The Challenge,* p. 29. He qualifies "noneconomic factors" as things basic for the functioning of the economy such as the attitudes and traditional institutions of society. With this in mind, Myrdal points to another fallacy of the development literature, that only quantifiable factors amenable to mathematical computation are "economic," and that it is sufficient to refer to them to describe the functioning of an economy, its defects and their remedies. Many nonsocialist economists are as captivated by this fallacy as are the fiercest devotees of central planning.
4. Ibid., pp. 44, 45.
5. Ibid., p. 49.
6. There is a paperback edition by Anchor Press/Doubleday (Garden City, N.Y., 1976).
7. From the early days of Spanish domination, in Mexico there was a legend that the apostle Thomas had made an evangelizing expedition to those lands and left the seed of Christianity and the prophecy of his return, which the Mexicans believed was fulfilled with the arrival of the Spaniards. A comparable mythical explanation has never been advanced as explanation of the conquest of Peru by Pizarro.
8. McNeil, *Plagues and People.*
9. Myrdal, *The Challenge,* p. 218.
10. Ibid., pp. 234, 235.
11. Ibid., p. 235.
12. Ibid.
13. Quoted in *Orientación Económica* (Caracas: Instituto Venezolano de Análisis Económico y Social, February 1966) no. 18, p. 17.
14. The same happened, with the differences due to the epoch and culture, one-and-a-half centuries before in Spanish America. Disconcerted by the deplorable result of political independence, in contrast with the unlimited hopes that had been placed upon it, the Spanish Americans soon (and long before Max Weber) began to attribute the frustration of their societies to the cultural differences between Protestant and Catholic countries (for example, the Chilean Francisco Bilbao, 1823-1865). About the same time it became fashionable to blame Indians, Blacks, the mixture of races, and to encourage white European immigration. Deprived of its racist connotations and reduced to its cultural meaning, this has an obvious foundation, but is insufficient and has an important component of bad faith to the degree that it attempts to exonerate the whites or near-whites, the Spanish American ruling classes. That explanation preceded the one that is fashionable today, which is that proposed by the Third World ideology.
15. *L'Express,* August 30, 1980.

9

Beyond Third World Ideology

The currently prevalent influence of the Third World ideology is one of the central as well as most ominous facts of contemporary history. On all sides we have the evidence that the adoption of socialism leads to a monstrous growth of the state, to the cornering and eventual suffocation of civil society, to authoritarianism and finally to totalitarianism. Although there are still people who believe in good faith that such evidence is not relevant to the advanced capitalist countries, where supposedly socialism could coexist with freedom, no one except fanatics or propagandists can deny it in relation to the poor and backward countries. The fact that such invariable results have not hindered the advance of the Third World Ideology forces one to ponder the future global prospects (and not only in the Third World) of the freedoms consubstantial with the civilization of capitalism.

According to the French poet Paul Claudel, man is not made for happiness. It could be that neither is he made for freedom and prosperity, and that socialism in its different forms, and of course in its Third World version, is the political result of that apparent anomaly. In any case, it seems to correspond perfectly to the lack of concern that traditional ruling classes (the priestly, clerical, and warrior castes, and in general, all those who in history have been privileged and have counted on continuing to be so) have shown for the welfare and the freedom of the common people, the plebians. Freedom and general prosperity, where they have grown as a result of the rise of a market economy have done so in spite of the aristocrats, the priests, and the intellectuals.

A different and much more disturbing phenomenon is the indifference of masses of people who have enjoyed the fruits of capitalism (plebians, a class whom the civilization of capitalism has largely rescued in the last 200 years from poverty and servitude) toward those advantages once they have become customary. Never before has the fable of the frogs requesting a king had such relevance.

To such people, the astounding improvement in their well-being that has taken place in the past forty years seems unremarkable or even insufficient, and at the same time has seemed without perceptible connection to the market economy that produced it and that has managed to absorb reasonably well the brutal blow of the tenfold increase in oil prices. Incapable of perceiving the incomparably more severe and moreover really perverse economic crisis of socialism, many disgruntled western Europeans and even North Americans tend to give fresh credit to the worn socialist allegation that only the market economy (capitalism) impedes the explosive flowering of the productive forces and that if their societies adopted some kind of democratic socialism the assured result would be the triumphal resumption of economic growth and guaranteed employment for all, working less and consuming more. It was with this absurd program that in France for example, socialism got a mandate to save that country from capitalism.

A Reactionary Nostalgia

Such blindness on such a scale cannot be explained as part of a passing phase. There must be something in capitalist civilization that is dissonant with our emotions; there must be something in socialism that harmonizes with them. Chafarevich[1] proposes that the perennial fascination with socialism, present in all utopian designs since Plato, has to respond to an irrational psychic requirement paradoxically disguised as exacerbated rationalism. Karl Popper[2] perceives a universal nostalgia for the tribal, static society, where the individual did not exist. In the open society, which has emerged gradually over the past ten or twelve thousand years, man is constantly forced to make personal decisions. We have not become used to this, the greatest revolution. Of course, our critical capacity has been freed and freedom has become, in theory, the supreme value; so much so that the tyrants assure that they will guarantee it. But we live under stress, insecurity, anxiety. We must at each step chose, question ourselves, discipline ourselves, adapt, compete, win and also lose. The shock of the transition from the tribal society to the open society, biologically very recent, has not been absorbed. Recognitions of the advantages of the open society stand out in history since Pericles, but also, since Plato, there has been a reactionary nostalgia for the tribal society. These latter are much more esteemed. Utopianism is generally considered to be morally virtuous and esthetically pleasant, in spite of the political monstrosities it has fathered in practice, including all the totalitarian experiments. On the other hand, libertarianism suffers from a certain lack of regard, because it is recognized as founded on the understanding that men are imperfect and takes that reality into account, instead of promising to bring forth a "new man," a "superman."

The socialist spirit is, then, literally reactionary. The true new man would be the one who could free himself from the bonds with the (recent) past when the human species was very similar to the other animals of prey who, because they hunt in packs, are, indeed, collectivist.

The apparent novelty of Marxist socialism is due to its coincidence and its correspondence with a situation unprecedented in history: industrial capitalist society. Before the capitalist revolution with its amazing productivity, human societies could not have pondered the extravagant idea that the severe poverty of the majority of their members could be alleviated. Even less would they worry about the poverty of other societies, the way today's prosperous nations are concerned with poverty of the Third World. The normal state of society was the level of subsistence, always close to disaster, perennially prisoner of what Galbraith has called the equilibrium of poverty. Not only misfortunes (drought, plague, war) but also any chance fortunate alteration (seven years of plenty, with the resulting decreased mortality and greater vulnerability to the next inevitable scarcity) meant disaster. Human life was in a permanent state of siege by forces outside of human control.

A community in mortal danger does not question the necessity of submitting to authoritarian government. A city surrounded by enemies welcomes ruthless leadership. Even in our time martial law is welcome after some catastrophe, and plunderers shot on sight. In many parts of the world this was and is the normal situation. It was the universal condition of mankind before capitalism created first a small surplus, and recently an immense surplus, above the subsistence level.

It was men of critical and rational (capitalist) minds living in unfortunate times of civil war or of foreign domination, men such as Hobbes and Machiavelli, who for the first time clearly said what everybody knew but was unutterable or perhaps too trite before the initiation of capitalist civilization: that the world is a dangerous and brutal place, and that given the scarcity of resources that was prevalent in Machiavelli's time (sixteenth century) or in Hobbes's time (seventeenth) century), men in a state of anarchy are condemned to fight like beasts among themselves, by which they cause others and bring unto themselves even more misery; and that is true for the relations among human groups; and that therefore groups without competent, strong leadership, are destined to be victims of effectively led groups. Of all the misfortunes that can befall a society, none is worse or more terrible than the violent internal strife of civil war. What little comfort and security men may hope for can take place only when the evils of anarchy and civil war have been replaced by the lesser evil of an authoritarian and implacable government.

To Change the World

It is no accident that those individuals (or classes) that for whatever reasons were capable of assuming the requried leadership extracted a high price for their services. A radical change that dethrones a ruling class is usually spurred by the judgment that those services were no longer being provided; and that change has invariably been led by those who could in turn reestablish the internal and external security of the society. Marxist economics excludes from its field of vision this purely political basis of the transference of power from one elite to another.

The precapitalist societies were traditionally governed by priestly castes in combination with military aristocracies, parasitical minorities that extorted an exorbitant proportion of the scarce social product. But this was, for the abused social body, the lesser evil, in comparison with the annihilation or reduction to slavery that would have been the consequences of a successful foreign assault.

Because in precapitalist society conditions of extremely low productivity could not find a better political solution than submission to an implacable authority, all precapitalist political thought had a tendency to revolve around ways of legitimizing that fact. Power was identified with godhead, and submission with piety. Any objection to the implicit hypocrisy, could not be political, but religious, and heterodox at that (since religious orthodoxy was a part of the system of social control) with the aspiration to justice transferred out of the secular to a different dimension. "My kingdom is not of this world" and "Give to Caesar what belongs to Caesar" are classical expressions of the genuine religious spirit in societies resigned to deep poverty and subject to the domination of such authorities. This did not dispense just citizens from the obligation to attempt to achieve justice, but not through the foolish ambition of pretending to change the world, but rather by the infinitely patient addition of acts of individual charity, whose sum would some day end up by literally making the false world of injustice disappear.

A Hassidic tale perfectly illustrates this attitude. Haskele decides to improve the world and asks himself where to begin. The whole world is too large; will he begin with his country? It would still be satanical ambition. Should he begin with the province, the district, the town, his street, his family? Each time Haskele realizes that there is a sinful presumption in pretending to be ready to improve others. The project of saving the world cannot be undertaken except through the humble, although infinitely difficult task of improving ourselves, trying to be just in all our acts.

Virtue Without Toil

The end of hopeless poverty and the rise of nationalism, both connected to the civilization of capitalism, produced a radical change in the direction and content of the aspiration to justice. There had always been secular, atheistic and agnostic spirits. But they could not seriously imagine or desire that a majority could be of a similar inclination, and this for strictly political reasons. How could society have been governed without the aid of religion? A sufficiently educated, prosperous and free person who harbored doubts about the truth of religious teachings might intimately feel that official religion was a political tool, but surely concluded that it was good that such was the case.

When the capitalist-rationalist-liberal revolution resulted in an amazing increase in wealth, it became possible for the first time to conceive of a secular society (neither utopian nor otherworldly) where justice and equality could be realized by the fair distribution of an effectively existing wealth. Individuals and groups inevitably emerged to preach that only imperfections due to traditional social organization perversely blocked such consummation. Moreover, they believed themselves to be so generous, so lacking in selfishness, and endowed with such intellectual power or with such a good education and restraint, that to expect that the same qualities could extend to the rest of mankind seemed reasonably conceivable to them. This would see the rise of a new socialist society, in which there would be no extremes of poverty or wealth, if not beatific equality, and no longer any need for state coercion to discourage or suppress the spontaneous violence that all prior historical experience had demonstrated exists potentially in societies, ready to burst forth upon any relaxation of the double threat of repression and hunger.

Such were the utopian socialists. The unrealistic thinking of these reformers is evidenced by the transparent impracticality of the ways they proposed to extend to all men the moral and intellectual qualities that they felt they themselves possessed.

Marxism fit perfectly with the spirit of the times when it was formulated, an epoch that had traded Christian historicism for the belief in progress, aggressively persuaded of the falseness of religion, but at the same time hungry for a "scientific" substitute for that emptiness. Karl Marx, the "scientific" socialist, understood the need for a practical "scientific" answer to the problems implicit in the aspiration to socialism. If, as Rousseau argued, man is by nature free and kind, and it is society that corrupts and enslaves him, there must be a secret spring which, if we knew how to unleash it, would return men to their primitive condition of goodness and natural freedom. If there was a fall, there can be redemption, virtue without toil, salvation by contagion and with it a happy end for the horror story of history. That magical secret spring is, naturally, the abolition of private property. In the *Communist Manifesto* we find the categorical affirmation that that measure, by itself, is socialism.

Marxism and Mythology

Marxism is not only clearly derivative of various currents of immediately prior thought (English political economy, German philosophy, French socialism) which Marx readily recognized but—and this Marx would not acknowledge—also incorporates a complex amalgam of ancient emotions, aspirations and frustrations that are at the root of permanent obsessions of the human spirit. Marxism comprises features of some of mankind's oldest and most persistent myths: the Golden Age, equivalent to that of the Earthly Paradise, which Marxism imagined existed before the history we know in the form of a communist state of society, a primitive period of natural harmony, goodness and innocence; the myth of the loss of that primitive beatitude (the fall) due to the accidental and perverse establishment of private property; and the myth of the millennium, which has certainly had a very curious place in the history of the ideas of the West.[4]

Millennialism is a variant of salvationism. Invariably, salvationist prophecies offer their fulfillment in the short term, and Marxism has not been an exception. But with the delay in the return of the messiah or the revolution or if one or the other event happens but does not yield the expected fruits, it becomes necessary to find explanations for that contingency and ways of maintaining the faith of the true believers. Thus, for example, in Christianity, the disciples' expectation that Christ would return within their lifetime was transformed into the cult of the Redeemer and the doctrine of the final judgement and the resurrection of the dead on that day.

Orthodox Christian doctrine also prophecied that Christ must return to found here on earth a kingdom of one thousand years. This doctrine was condemned by the Church as a heresy. But there must be something in it attuned to human yearnings, because millennialism has been a recurring phenomenon, and not only in the fanatical passions of heretical religious sects, but also in the mystical background of revolutionary political ideas.[5]

In the thirteenth century, the millennialism of Joachim de Fiore was the most influential prophetic system known in Europe before Marxism. From the traditional idea that the Holy Scriptures have an arcane meaning, de Fiore audaciously thought that that secret sense could be a key to understanding and predicting the development of history. Through an interpretation of the Bible he formulated a historicism that consisted of supposing the development of human affairs to be a progress through three ages, the last of which would be, with relation to the first two, like summer compared to spring and winter. The first age had been one of ignorance and fear, the second of faith and submission, and the third would be one of freedom, joy and love.

That Joachimite historicism of the three ages found echoes in the thought of German philosophers Lessing, Schelling, Fichte, and Hegel, and in the theory of Auguste Comte on the evolution of history through the theological, metaphysical, and scientific stages. Likewise, the Marxist hypothesis sets forth three stages of social development: primitive communism (before the fall), the class society, and the return of communism through the proletarian revolution, when antagonisms would cease, freedom would reign, and man would be converted into a superman. The adoption by Hitler of the expression "Third Reich" to describe his project of German hegemony for a thousand years had its roots in the same folkloric fantasy that history is advancing toward that third stage of glory and happiness.

A characteristic of millennialism is that its goals and promises are unlimited. The exertion of millennialist militants is not seen as the way toward reasonable and specific reformist objectives but rather as a prelude to an event of unique importance, different from all other mutations that have occurred in history, a cataclysm from which the world will emerge radically transformed, completely changing human life. Such proselytizing holds fantastic and powerful appeal especially for the downtrodden, who cannot fail to find in it at once a consolation, an immediate emotional compensation, a promise of revenge, and a salvationist prospect answering one of the most unquenchable desires of human beings.

Outbursts of medieval millennialism occurred when a prophet would appear, endowed with personal magnetism and charisma, lending plausibility to his pretense of being fated to play a special role in the imminent conclusion of history. His was not the mediocre offer to improve somewhat the lives of those who followed him, but rather the opportunity of being among the few elected to carry out a mission of incomparable importance.

The immediate followers of the prophet were a group that would acquire a force of conviction and of compulsion, a zeal, an energy, a lack of consideration for the normal concerns of human beings that would empower them to excite and gather much larger groups of disoriented, perplexed, aggrieved individuals, who found in the prophet and his fanatic nucleus of followers a new master worth submitting to. In our own time the fascists and Nazis used that scheme, but much more rigorously and earlier, the Bolsheviks. It is significant that while the medieval mlllennialist movements excited and mobilized the dullest and most ignorant peasants, they lacked appeal for the craftsmen organized in guilds. In the same way in our time Marxism-Leninism has been singularly incapable of seducing the industrial workers of the West (with the exception of a dwindling labor sector of France and Italy); at the same time, however, it has fed the fantasies of violent and final revolution that will drown capitalism in blood which fascinate both Third World ideologists such as Fidel Castro or Muammar Qadhafi, and, in the very heart of the West, those who are so disaffected by capitalist civilization that they dream of seeing the Third World turn into an assault force against their own societies.

Third World Ideology Once Again

By a different way we have again found the Third World ideology and its link with socialism in our epoch. Millennialism is capable of firing the imagination of the poor and humiliated countries of the world with an emotional satisfaction unequalled by any rational project or doctrine. Furthermore, in its daily running of government in communist countries, socialism has proved itself in a way that contributes greatly and perhaps decisively to its prestige. It has confronted without idealism or sentimentality (and without humanitarianism or charity, according to this point of view) the political problems inherent in a revolution so against nature in its advocacy of the abolition of private property. The solution has consisted, as we well know, in the establishment of implacable totalitarian dictatorship, so that in actual practice, though starting from the fuzzy nostalgias of salvationism and millennialism, socialism ends up by offering a rationality, and a method perfected in its smallest detail to establish, maintain, and justify

autocracies that would leave even Hobbes breathless. A sincere socialist could argue, if he were to put his cards on the table and assume as a
virtue the totalitarian logic of socialism, that such a result has a
marvelous relevancy for the problems that afflict the Third World. This
hypothetical sincere socialist could even accept the falsehood of the
Third World ideology and go on to argue that some regions of the Third
World (not always the poorest or most unfortunate) are perhaps
radically adverse to a tolerably successful adaptation of the complex of
incentives to free human action that have yielded such an excellent
result not only in the central Western countries, but also wherever the
previously existing culture proved capable of assimilating capitalist
civilization. There would prevail in those regions of the Third World a
perhaps unsurmountable combination of dead weight (the ancient
customs and traditional institutions itemized by Gunnar Myrdal) and
the wholly recent intoxication caused by the Third World ideology.
Therefore, our hypothetical sincere socialist would conclude a ruthless
government is required, as in our time only socialists are capable of
providing.

For those who might think that I am joking, I will relate a polemic in
France between socialists. One of them, Jacques Julliard, wrote an
article called "The Third World and the Left" *(Le tiers monde et la
gauche)*[6] and another Guy Sitbon, replied *(Le temps des méprises):*

> I well know that we live in times inclined to anarchism—which is
> nice and rather comforting—so that it is in fashion to accuse the
> State of all evils. But we are not forced to surrender completely to
> this fad and, for example, it is well to ask if in 1939, when facing
> Nazi Germany, a powerful French State would not have been
> useful. . . . There was once a country where the rights of man
> were respected. Where freedom of the press was perfect. Its
> parliament was one of the liveliest in the Third World. Freedom in
> that country was all the greater since the police and the Army
> were weak. But then a foreign army infiltrated Lebanon, and after
> another, and still another. . . .
>
> There are no longer many human rights in Lebanon, but there are
> many Syrian soldiers, happy to be citizens of a Nation-State that
> is more powerful and less liberal.[7]

I trust that the reader is as amazed as I am by Sitbon's statement. It
is totally false that our times lean toward "anarchism," if by this we
mean (as does Sitbon) healthy distrust of the liberal spirit toward state

power and the men and the institutions that embody it. The truth is exactly the opposite, and its proof is Guy Sitbon's regret that opposite Nazi Germany, France in 1939 did not have a comparably powerful state, by which he means (and I am not putting words in his mouth) more soldiers and policemen and fewer freedoms.

We do not live, then, in times that lean toward anarchism (liberal democracy) but rather we are back, after a very brief interlude following the war against the fascist axis, to the fascination with military power and scorn for "decadent bourgeois democracy" that has characterized our century since the triumph of socialism in Russia in 1917. The victory of the democracies over fascism appears in this perspective as an historical anomaly, a kind of accident due above all to the unsuspected vitality of the United States in 1941, bought at the exorbitant price of preserving and legitimizing the Soviet Union, the greatest and most virulent source of antiliberalism, and yielding to it half of Europe. Today, a few years after that time, and in spite of the realization of what happens where socialism has been scrupulously realized, antiliberalism continues to rise, and the ability of socialism to whip society into step and to extirpate anarchism (neither more nor less than the promises of fascism) is heralded as the greatest of its virtues. Moreover, this socialism proposes to be not only a remedy for the unhappy Third World, but also a savior of the rotten Western democracies.

Capitalism's Unpardonable Sin

The Marcusian accusation against capitalist civilization that it is actually repressive or even "cryptofascist" is a transparent lie. Since Marcuse's ephemeral glory in 1968, it has shrunk into at most the obsession of the pathological left, as with the Red Brigades. One of the signal services rendered to socialism by the Third World ideology has been to give ground to the argument that capitalist civilization is not repressive where it flourishes only because it has transferred to the Third World the violence and cruelty supposedly consubstantial with capitalism and greater in this system than in any other. In the context of the same polemic provoked by Julliard's article, Régis Debray wrote a perfect compendium of the Third World ideology in 2,000 words, appropriately titled "Free Men Need Slaves" *(Il faut des esclaves aux hommes libres)*. According to Debray, Western Europe is "a privileged land in public freedom and material prosperity," but only because there exists a Third World "whose permanent exploitation is what guarantees the maintenance of those freedoms [in Western Europe]."[8]

If it were true that the French society and state are essentially the product of the relations of exploitation and oppression that France has maintained with the Third World, and if we were to admit, moreover, that there exists a relation of causality between the absence of freedom in the Third World and the existence of those same freedoms in France, that would be a compelling reason in favor of the thesis that the French socialist government in which Debray has played an important role should have attempted to cleanse the French economy and bring it down to its true nonimperialist floor. Of course, having reached that point, it would have become necessary to suspend the domestic liberties that France so abusively enjoys.

Surprisingly, Debray does not shrink from that logical consequence of his argument. According to him, if the French ceased living in civil peace and reasonable prosperity only supposedly at the expense of the Third World, then "here (in France) growth industries would stop on their tracks, factories would close, essential tropical products would have to be rationed. We would see unemployment spread, housewives take to the streets with their pots empty, workers fighting the police. Death in the street. The comrades of these victims would return the blows. There would be massive arrests, censorship, suspension of the political parties. The government would declare a state of emergency to defend the security of the citizens and the higher interests of the Nation. Human rights would disappear."[9]

Of this silly tirade, let us underline the confession of a rabid socialist that advanced capitalist societies are "privileged lands of public freedom and material prosperity." It appears that, to the reactionary socialist spirit that we all share to some degree, freedom and prosperity are the radical defects of those societies, the unforgivable flaw for which socialism appears to be the cure.

To those who know how to read the meaning of the long-run growth curves of the capitalist economies worthy of that name, it has become clear that the market economy is a formidable mechanism for the creation of wealth that functions, in the long run, with surprising regularity. On the other hand it has become totally obvious, for those who do not persist in deceiving themselves, that capitalist civilization by no means tends to fascism. On the contrary, with its abundance and tolerance it has made freedom, for the first time, an article for mass consumption. What the little reactionary socialist worm of remorse that wiggles within each one of us (the same that tormented Plato) asks is: can human society maintain itself at once free and stable if its members individually have, or think they have, the means and the right to behave precisely as they wish? According to the increasingly clear implications of the social contract that is characteristic of advanced capitalist civilization, we see the apparently inexorable advance of that tendency, and also of another: the inclination of each special interest to hold up the rest of the society by any means, which can be demanding entitlement in exchange for block votes, or striking by doctors, firemen, policemen, or garbage collectors (Labor disputes are still not legal but they are foreseeable even in the armed forces—there is already a soldiers' labor union in the Netherlands, and it is inevitable that the example will spread).

Characteristically, the events of May 1968 in France ended with a general salary increase. The small reactionary socialist worm in our innards reminds us that May 1968 has been described as a "carnival of the consumer society" and whispers the following terrible thought: capitalist civilization, leaving aside the fact of its dangerous coexistence with the socialist camp and the Third World, perhaps carries its own death in the paradox that its virtues, prosperity and freedom, tend to extinguish virtue in man.

The Besieged City

The countries of capitalist civilization are being confronted and virtually besieged by a still imperfect but already operational coalition between the socialist empire and the Third World, and the besiegers have within the threatened citadel an active, numerous, impune and even prestigious and influential "fifth column."

This expression comes from the Spanish Civil War, when the Francoist commander of the siege of Madrid, disposing of four military columns to carry out the siege of the city, boasted of counting on a fifth column of secret sympathizers within Madrid itself. The socialist fifth column in the West is not very secret, and runs less risks the more centrally it acts (in the major world centers of Paris, Frankfurt, or Milan). This fifth column enjoys legal status, as is just and fitting according to the rules of the game of capitalist civilization, unless some of its soldiers, (at their own discretion, and never that of the besieged) chose violent confrontation. While socialists criticize capitalist civilization for its supposed repressiveness, some of them systematically abuse the judicial guarantees and the unprecedented laxness of police control that the advanced capitalist societies offer.

Besides outright terrorism we see things happen that are in fact deliberately fostered as revolutionary, that are superficially discounted, judged to be nonpolitical or accidental, through an unsuspecting media carrying misinformation.[10]

There has been a vast increase in the drug trade. Education is assaulted through rejection of academic standards described as fascist. Even movements that are necessary and in many ways admirable, such as civil rights, women's rights, and ecologism, are manipulated by socialists and even generated from nothing, not to improve the situation of blacks or women or of defending the environment but rather to accelerate the dissolution of Western society or to affect its economic viability. This latter point is, clearly, the case of the campaign against nuclear energy. The agitation against nuclear power that the socialist "fifth column" actively carries out in the heart of the West (the besieged city) or in the Third World does not exist or is savagely repressed within the frontiers of the socialist empire.[11]

Within the same universe, although in another dimension, is terrorism. Few naive souls remain who still believe that there is no relation between the socialist camp and the rise of terrorism in the West and carefully chosen areas of the Third World, or who suppose that the attempt against the Pope's life was perpetrated by an assassin of "the right." Right wing terrorism does not have the characteristics of an international network. It operates randomly and locally, without strategic goals. It would be an exaggeration to suppose that the Soviet Union pulls all the strings of international terrorism. The KGB can occasionally conceive and order a specific murder. But it is obvious that the Soviet Union is generally concerned more with stimulating and assisting with training, money, weapons, false documents, clandestine or diplomatic safe houses, whatever psychopathic assassin or fanatical nationalist is ready to throw away his or her life and those of others. The only requirement to qualify for Soviet aid directly or through surrogates such as Cuba, Libya, North Korea or the Palestine Liberation Organization, is that it will wreak havoc in the heart of Western society. The connection of the respected and influential sectors of the socialist fifth column with terrorism emerge from time to time; witness the solicitude of Jean-Paul Sartre for the Baader-Meinhof Band, or the concern of prominent members of the French Socialist party for Klaus Croissant, a German lawyer who specializes in defending terrorists in court, and who in some way ran afoul of French law.

The Real Argument in Favor of Socialism

With all this, the whisper in our ear of the small socialist worm becomes terribly persuasive. The open, pluralist, changing, competitive (and because of this free and antidogmatic) society is admirable, but in actual practice turns out to be unequal to the wild aspirations and behavior patterns it arouses. Freed from the elementary struggle for existence, educated and informed, men do not become less, but rather more demanding. Socialism then arises as an answer, in appearance rational and reasonable, to what is perceived as an intolerable situation by prosperous free men: social inequality, the suffering of the weak, injustice, and even existential anguish. The economic and political achievements of the capitalist and industrial revolution, which are the highest achievements of the open society, create within it a tendency toward disintegration. Athenian democracy already turned out to be self-destructive; the Roman republic quickly became a monarchy, almost immediately hereditary, and later almost totally similar to the Oriental despotisms. Perhaps those precedents are a preview of our own future. It is unfortunately conceivable that the capitalist economies, with their corollary of political democracy, known by the world in the last two hundred years will eventually prove equally incapable of surmounting the double challenge of their own internal tensions (exacerbated by socialist criticism and subversion, which make the democracies increasingly difficult to govern) and of the military pressure of the modern Spartas, the socialist countries. It could well happen that in this, the first industrial and technological historical cycle, the open society may be cornered and finally destroyed by socialism, and that in this way the first moment of the Marxist prophecy would be fulfilled: capitalism will have opened the way to another "mode of production," in the same way that capitalism replaced feudalism.

But it is illusory that such a resolution of the present internal and external challenges against the open society, if indeed it came to pass, would lead to a classless society, where the freedom of all would be the condition of the freedom of each, and we should see the end of the exploitation of man by man, according to Marxist salvationism. What we would see, rather, is the reiteration of the socialist experience accumulated up to the present, and that such hypothetical triumph of socialism, if such is the direction that history is taking, would mean the generalization of a particularly perverse, technocratic form of what Marx discerned as characteristic of traditional Oriental societies: "the Asian mode of production," the subordination of society to the state, the exploitation of all workers by a bureaucratic class that perpetuates itself by selecting the most astute and cynical young people of each new generation, and, of course, by inheritance. And the state would be incarnated in the form of a person, a monarch with superhuman characteristics, a semi-God, for which there are more than enough examples in Stalin, Mao, Castro, Ceausescu or Kim Il Sung.

There is nothing new under the sun. Beyond the Third World ideology, which was our starting point, we see that there once again appears, now with the mask of socialism, Hobbes's awesome giant with his eternal enigmatic smile. Hatched from the theoretical work of Marx and delivered by the hands of Lenin and Stalin, the leviathan is reborn.

It is not even, as has been said, that Leninism-Stalinism is the painful path, difficult but necessary toward the socialist millennium, but rather that socialist theory opens the way to Leninism-Stalinism, and that therein lies its secret its and force. Socialism proposes the theoretical justification and the practical guidelines for building the leviathan corresponding to our epoch, the only possible contemporary way of snaring peoples into submitting to a new form of absolutism, not only in the unhappy Third World (which is only an instrument) but where it truly matters and counts: in the great industrial countries of the West.

That is the true argument in favor of socialism, inscribed not in words but in flagrant facts: its appeal as a substitute religion and its capacity to coerce. Socialist dictatorships have not arisen to promote and protect the humanist values proclaimed by socialism, but rather socialism and its humanistic references have been and will continue to be the excuse for setting up and maintainig totalitarian dictatorships.

The manifold problems of society are not therefore solved. But socialism restores desirable (indispensible?) disdain for the governed on the part of the rulers, the power of intimidation, and the distance its majestic governments keep from the governed. Contrast this with the guilt-ridden concern for the governed, the enfeebling familiarity and the unrepressive nature of democratic (bourgeois) governments, the lack of correspondence of democracy with the requirements of majestic administration. This can lead to the tortured attempt to prove that, since socialism is inevitable, perhaps it is not intolerable and would suggest that the fundamental weakness of capitalism resides in the fact that it is antiheroic and politically inept. The central protagonist of capitalist civilization, the business entrepreneur, completely lacks the virtues of the political leader. He does not walk about in hero's costume, like the military. He has no secret pact with God, like priests. He does not inspire fear. He is constitutionally incapable of demagogy. He does not despise economics. Waste, and even more the destruction of wealth horrify him. The only way he has of computing gains and losses is in terms of money (hence Lenin's prophecy: "They will sell us the rope by which we shall hang them.") If Napoleon had had half of such archetypical entrepreneurial traits he would have passed his life as a shopkeeper in Corsica. This is why business entrepreneurs have never really governed. At best, and at the peak of their power, they have sponsored politicians to govern for them. On their part, the politicians, a human type radically opposed to the entrepreneur, instinctively see in socialism a system that suits them perfectly, where all social life is politicized and the business person, that myopic, cowardly and miserly nuisance, has no place, or at most survives precariously, dethroned, humiliated, reduced to the status of servant of politics.

It is true that socialism does not produce general welfare and it rather reduces to poverty previously wealthy countries—but that could be one of the keys to its stability, once it achieves its Marxist-Leninist-Stalinist form. On the other hand it does invariably produce the phenomenon coyly called the "cult of the personality," the modern equivalent of the God-kings that human society seems to miss, which is absent from the theory but rabidly present in the practice of socialism. An unmistakable sign of the true nature of socialism is that the relationship between the socialist monarch (always a superman, except in moments of transition, interregnum or regency) and the governed is not institutional, is not based on formal delegation of power and the exercise of authority within the law, but is rather, presumably, a love affair in which leader and people are a single entity and the leader is always beyond error because he is capable of interpreting at each moment the profound desires and the true interests of the masses.

In conclusion, the promise of progress that socialism offers us, which has already been fulfilled for a certain number of countries is, "Beyond freedom and dignity"—those two conditions created or at least unprecedentedly enhanced by capitalism.[12]

Notes

1. Igor Chafarevich, *Le Phénomène socialiste* (Paris: Seuil, 1977).
2. Karl Popper, *The Open Society and its Enemies* (Princeton: Princeton University Press, 1966).
3. J. K. Galbraith defines this as a situation in which an increase in the welfare of a population unchains developments (for example, lower infant mortality) that will end by counterbalancing the improvement, and restoring poverty to the previous level.
4. See Norman Cohn, *The Pursuit of the Millenium* (London: Paladin, 1970).
5. In Chapter 2 we referred to the communist experiment in Münster led by Jan Matthys and Jan Bockelson.
6. *Le Nouvel Observateur* 708 (June 5, 1978).
7. Ibid., 713 (July 10, 1978).
8. *Le Monde Diplomatique,* October 1978. The several articles provoked by this polemic were gathered in one volume by Seuil, Paris, 1979, with the

title of the article by Julliard that lit the fuse, *Le Tiers Monde et La Gauche*.

9. From the article previously quoted in *Le Monde Diplomatique* (October 1978).

10. See Claire Sterling, *The Terror Network: The Secret War of International Terrorism* (New York: Holt, Rinehart, & Winston, 1981).

11. It is said that trees never grow up to the sky, and it is true that the Soviet Union has its own problems, from which the West can derive relief. For example, the geopolitical rivalry with China, that so worries the Soviets, Afghanistan's stubborn resistance, Polish rebelliousness and the tensions and internal contradictions of the Soviet Union. But the Soviet Government will surely become more and not less aggressive to the degree that it confronts problems of the system and of the empire, and the rapproachement of China to the West, even if we suppose it to be lasting, is too reminiscent of the Western alliance with the Soviet Union against Nazi Germany.

12. B. F. Skinner, *Beyond Freedom and Dignity* (London: Cape, 1972).

Index

Afghanistan, 61n1
Agriculture, 131-33
Argentina, 45, 47-50, 67, 102n12. *See also* Latin America
Asia, 144-46. *See also* name of country
Autarchy, 96-98
Authoritarianism, socialist spirit of, 119-20, 158, 159, 161, 162-63, 166-67, 173-74

Bauer, P. T., 81, 86n13
Bazil, Beatrice, 109
Belgium, 91
Bockelson, Jan, 33n4
Bolivia, 94-95. *See also* Latin America
Boulding, Kenneth, 86n11
Bourgeoisie: achievements of, 15n5; basis of, 17n9; Engels' views about, 35n7, 85n9; importance of, 15n5, 85n9; Social Democracy/Democratic Socialism and, 23-24
Brain drain, 71-72, 73, 85n7
Brandt Commission, 138-39
Britain. *See* Great Britain

Capitalism: agriculture and, 131-33; arguments against, 111-18, 168-79; beneficiaries of, 107-10; British, 99-102; cities and, 118-20; consumption and, 11, 12, 17n8; creativity of, 9-10, 135; definition of, 107; disintegration of, 172; growth of, 8-11, 77; imperialism and, 1, 125, 143-44; industrialization and, 53, 125-31; "late competitors" of, 75-77; liberalism and, 105-7, 120n1; market economy of, 169-70; nature of, 105-23; poverty and, 79-81; productivity of, 11, 17n8; Protestant reformation and, 98-99; qualities worth emulating of, 98-101; revolution of, 89-104; Schumpeter on, 9-11; socialism and, 8-9, 11-12, 113-18, 160-62; Third World and, 11-12, 65-87, 96-97; trade and, 66-67, 85n9; tyrants and, 92-97, 103n12; wars and, 1, 114-15. *See also* Capitalist civilization; Europe; West
Capitalist civilization, 106-7, 110-15, 120, 160-62, 168-70
Chafarevich, Igor, 160
Che Guevara, 64n13
Chile, 73, 84n6. *See also* Latin America
China, 3-5
Christianity, 53, 98-99, 104n13, 164-65
Cities, growth of, 118-20
Class struggle, 25-26
Climate, influence of, 146-47
Clock, importance of, 127-29
Colonialism, xi-xii, 1, 12n1, 39-42, 55-57, 79, 90-92
Communism, ix-x, xi, 6-7, 116. *See also* Marxism; Socialism; Soviet Union
Communist Manifesto (Marx and Engels), 8, 11, 31, 110, 164
Competition, 43
Consumption and capitalism, 11, 12, 17n8
Cuba, 45, 46, 50, 70, 71

Debray, Regis, 168-69
Democratic Socialism, 23-24
Demonstration effect, 70-71
Dependence, theory of, 73, 90
Development, xi-xiii, 38-39, 47, 51-55
Disease, 147-50
Dominance. *See* Capitalism; West

East Germany. *See* Germany
Ecology, anticapitalist, 116-18, 123n17
Education, mass, 53

177